DATE DUE			
Feb 28 '75 Rd			
May 19 '75			
Apr 26 79			

BORN TO PLAY BALL

Willie Mays has been cheered enthusiastically in and out of the ball parks where he has played. He has been called the greatest natural player of all time. Now, finally, Willie speaks for himself in a book that will delight his fans of all ages. Not only the story of his life is included, for Willie gives many tips on batting form, fielding and throwing.

BORN
TO PLAY BALL

by Willie Mays

AS TOLD TO

CHARLES EINSTEIN

G. P. PUTNAM'S SONS
NEW YORK

MANUFACTURED IN THE UNITED STATES OF AMERICA
Van Rees Press • New York

Contents

Illustrations will be found following page 108.

Introduction

WHY WILLIE?

WHAT passes for the miraculous in baseball has occurred twice in our time. In 1951, the New York Giants came on to win the National League pennant after trailing the Brooklyn Dodgers by thirteen and one-half games on August 11, a kind of stretch-run unparalleled in the annals of the game. In 1954, the New York Giants again won the pennant, this time after having finished thirty-five games out of the lead the season before (once again, a recovery unmatched in baseball history). More in the character of the straight, unalloyed baseball miracle, however, the Giants went on, not only to defeat the favored Cleveland Indians in the world series, but to do it in four straight games. The shock effect was heightened immeasurably by the fact that the Giants not only beat the Indians—they beat the bejabbers out of them.

It will have to be left to history to decide once and for all the true significance of the role played in the development of these baseball miracles by Willie Mays, whose book this is. It will be left to history if a nation of baseball fans in general, and Giant fans in particular, care to wait that long. Many of them do not so choose. They already have stamped Mays as the greatest ballplayer of all time. No such verdict can be delivered temperately, especially in view of the fact that 1954 was Mays's first full season in the big leagues and that the season was well under way before the young man observed his twenty-third birthday. But the most fanatic of Mays's fans can show an extraordinary amount of evidence to support their claims.

In is a fact, for example, that Mays is the only player in the history of baseball whose big league reputation was established before his first complete season in the majors. This can be attributed in no uncertain fashion to that one universal table of statistics which finds itself daily in every newspaper in the United States, whether or not the location boasts any big league enthusiasm. That is the standing of the teams. It works this way:

Mays missed about the first quarter of the 1951 season. He was called up then from Minneapolis by the New York Giants, who were still dismally trying to untrack from the aftereffects of an eleven-game losing streak. Willie hit .274 for the Giants, a figure that wins no cigars. The Giants won the pennant.

In 1952, Mays had played less than one-quarter of the season before the Army drafted him. He was hitting a mere .236 at the time. But the Giants were in first place. They did not stay there after Willie left. They finished a dispirited second. In 1953, without Mays again, they tailed off woefully to fifth place.

It is, perhaps, understandable that when Willie rejoined the Giants in time for the 1954 season, he was already something of a myth. By some mysterious alchemy, the Giants now were supposed to win the pennant.

This, of course, they did.

But the mystery of Willie Mays's influence on the Giants goes considerably deeper than the standings. A center fielder, in the usual sense, is selected primarily for his hitting prowess, not because fielding is unimportant at that position, but because there are always a dozen other men ready to step into his shoes. Mays is regarded generally as a better fielder than he is a hitter. That is true today, even though in 1954 he won the National League batting cham-pionship with a mark of .345, scoring well over 100 runs, batting in well over 100 runs, hitting 41 home runs, leading his league in three-base hits, setting a new Giant record for extra-base hits (his total of 87 eclipsed a twenty-five-year-old record set by a fair hand named Mel Ott), and compil-ing the unlikely "slugging average" of .667. The "slugging average," an unusually revealing phase of that wild melange called baseball statistics, is obtained by dividing a player's total bases (four for a home run, three for a triple, two for a double, one for a single) by the number of times he came to bat. In 565 at-bats, Mays had 377 total bases.

Indeed, greatness in the outfield demands good hitting. Of the four players who inevitably wind up in anybody's "all-time" outfield—Babe Ruth in right, Ty Cobb in left, Tris Speaker and/or Joe DiMaggio in center—all four were great hitters. None made his primary mark as a fielder—not, at least, when separated into the categories of fielder and hitter—though all four were accomplished de-fensive men. As center fielders, where the comparison with

Mays most likely engages, Speaker and DiMaggio both possessed the ability to range far. It is no mean talent. Mays has it. There have been many great throwers among center fielders, among, in fact, outfielders in general. Daniel M. Daniel, a baseball writer whose experience goes back two generations, says Mays has the greatest arm in the history of the game.

Yet outfielding is not just catching and throwing. The fielding of ground balls; the instinct—an actual inborn instinct which DiMaggio once said must be there for an outfielder to be great defensively—to move with the swinging of the bat some three hundred feet away; the ability to throw to the right base—behind the runner, if necessary; the talent to play rebounds—all of these are facets of the outfielder's job.

But if a manager were given an outfielder who was good in all separate respects, and could choose one respect in which the same outfielder would be truly great—then, beyond doubt, that one respect would be the speed with which the outfielder gets rid of the ball. There is no involved or complicated reasoning behind this. Baseball is played in the infield. That is where the base runners are. The outfielder who can get the ball away faster than his fellows is a man among men.

In this respect, Willie Mays is a shining star. His catch of a drive by Vic Wertz of Cleveland in the first game of the 1954 world series, a catch which Cleveland manager Al Lopez said afterwards broke the Indians' back, was made monumental by the fact that, running full tilt with his back turned to the infield, at a point 460 feet from home plate, he got the ball back so fast that the man on second base made it only to third, instead of to home plate as could well have been expected, while the man on first base did not dare advance at all! This happened in the eighth inning, with the score tied, two men on, and nobody out.

There is a difference of opinion on what was Mays's "greatest" play in the outfield. A catch on Bob Skinner of Pittsburgh in 1954, a throw on Joe Cunningham of St. Louis the same season, a throw on Billy Cox of Brooklyn in 1951—all certainly rate high. Mays himself declines to compare fielding plays. "It ain't a play unless you catch it," he has said, and what he meant by that was that some of the toughest plays he has had to make have gone overlooked by the press and public. He himself, for example, says that his big play in the 1954 world series was not the catch he made on Wertz, but his holding Wertz to two bases on a vicious hit that rolled past the distant left-field bull pen two innings later. And it is a fact that this play went utterly unnoticed by writers and fans.

Statistics are no help at all in comparing outfielders. If an outfielder makes only a few assists in a season, it can mean either that he was unable to get runners with his arm or that, conversely, runners were unwilling to give him the chance by trying for the extra base.

Valid comparisons can be made in the field of hitting, however, on the basis of statistics. There is some conflict among fans and writers as to which season should be considered Mays's first in the majors—1951, when he missed approximately the first quarter of the campaign, or 1954. Mays himself says 1951 was his first year. On the other hand, it could be taken as unfair to Willie to compare his

1951 season to the freshman seasons of other outfielding greats, because his previous experience in organized ball was so limited when contrasted with theirs.

What does seem fair is to select a player's first season in which he appeared in 125 games or more of big league competition. The following table undertakes to compare Willie Mays with the six acknowledged all-time greats among outfielders—Ruth, Cobb, Speaker, DiMaggio, Ted Williams, and Stan Musial—at the equivalent times in their careers, *i.e.*, their first big league seasons of 125 games or more.

The categories used for comparative purposes include number of games, number of times at bat, number of hits, number of home runs, number of total bases, batting average, and slugging average. There are many other categories, but they seem without value. Runs-batted-in, for example, depends to too much a degree on the run-producing ability of the entire team to be applicable to seven different players on seven different teams in seven different years. The same holds true of runs scored.

This is the table:

Name	*Bats*	*Team*	*Year*	*G*	*AB*	*H*	*HR*	*TB*	*B.A.*	*SL.A.*
Tris Speaker	L	Boston AL	1909	143	544	168	7	241	.309	.443
Stan Musial	L	St. Louis NL	1942	140	467	147	10	229	.315	.490
Babe Ruth	L	Boston AL	1919	130	432	139	29	284	.322	.657
Joe DiMaggio	R	New York AL	1936	138	637	206	29	367	.323	.576
Ted Williams	L	Boston AL	1939	149	565	185	31	344	.327	.609
Willie Mays	R	New York NL	1954	151	565	195	41	377	.345	.667
Ty Cobb	L	Detroit AL	1907	150	605	212	5	286	.350	.473

As can be seen, the seven men have been listed in increasing order according to batting average. By chance, the proximity of Mays and Ted Williams offers an unusual opportunity for spot comparison, because both came to bat 565 times. Mays got ten more hits and ten more homers than Williams!

It is suspected that this table of statistics can supply considerable fuel to fan discussions; as an added thought in that direction, it can be said that Musial, DiMaggio, Mays, and Cobb were with pennant-winners in their "first" years; Speaker, Ruth, and Williams were not.

All heretics, assemble here.

It is logical to assume that if one man can mean as much to a ball club as is claimed for Mays, then the club will rise and fall depending upon that man's day-to-day performance. It may be logical, but it won't wash. The Giants have won when Mays was not hitting and lost when he was; lost when he made the great play in the field and won when he didn't. More often, to be sure, they have depended upon him to an extreme degree.

The point being made here is a suggestive one—that Mays's value to his team is made of stuff that includes, but vividly transcends, his ability to hit and field. Many men have tried to put this quality into words. Charley Grimm, manager of the Milwaukee Braves, has said, "He can help a team just by riding on a bus with them."

George Jessel, the comedian, said, "It's possible at this rate that even Willie Mays will be forgotten in two thousand years." Jessel said this upon learning that a great many Italians never heard of Julius Caesar.

Mays's own manager, Leo Durocher, says simply that Mays is "the greatest player I ever laid eyes on." From another source—Jack Hardy, a shortstop who played against Mays in the Negro National League—came an honest appraisal, limited to two words: "Willie's unbelievable."

Hardy recalls the first time he played against Mays—who was then sixteen or seventeen years of age. "He made a throw on a runner coming home after a fly ball," Hardy said, "and it was a heller. Boy, we landed on him. We called him lucky and every other name in the book. You ain't lived till you've heard the bench jockeys in colored ball.

"Willie? He didn't say nothing. He just went out there next inning and made a better throw on a faster runner. The hell with it. We keep our mouths shut."

Mays is, essentially, an exciting ballplayer to watch—and that, in turn, is intrinsic, and not just because he happened along in an era of unexciting ballplayers. He himself is excited about baseball. Roughly, but not unfondly, a friend from his barnstorming days has said, "Willie? He don't drink. He don't smoke. The only thing he ever done that was wrong was take a bath. He likes baseball."

Mays does like baseball. He transmits his excitement instantly to the spectator. It is a characteristic difficult to trace—one that has been defined loosely as *color*. Lawton Carver, the proprietor of Camillo's Restaurant in New York, covered baseball for a quarter of a century, most of it as the sports editor of the International News Service, and developed an interesting theory on the matter of color in a ballplayer. Carver's theory divided the great colorful players of baseball into two categories. One concerned the type of player who could be expected to make news of some kind off the field as well as on, or in some on-the-field by-product of the game as well as in the game itself. Ruth, Cobb, Williams, Dizzy Dean, and Jackie Robinson would belong to this category.

The other element comprised those stars whose appeal stemmed only from the way they played baseball. You could not take your eyes off Carl Hubbell when he pitched, or Walter Johnson, or Bob Feller.

Willie Mays fits into this second category. He is something to watch on the field. Listen to the buzz of expectation when he comes to bat. Watch his actions, his movements (Gilbert Millstein, in a superb article on Mays in the New York Sunday *Times*, said Mays was Rousseau's Natural Man). Willie stands five feet, ten and one-half inches; he weighs about 180 pounds. He has big hands, splendid muscles.

He is, to the real connoisseur of baseball, the ballplayer incarnate. To him has been paid the tribute supreme: he strikes out beautifully. That has been said of only one other player in all baseball history. That other player was Babe Ruth.

And yet, unlike Ruth, Mays is exciting on the field and not off. This despite his record number of appearances on various television shows; his well-known predilection for playing stickball on the streets of Harlem; his featured presentation in *Collier's, Life, Look, Newsweek, Time*, and the good Lord only knows where else.

INTRODUCTION

It was unprecedented for president Horace Stoneham of the Giants to place the kind of advertisement he did in the Minneapolis papers when the Giants called Mays up from the Minneapolis team in 1951. Said Stoneham of Mays, who had never played an inning of big league ball. "This player's exceptional talents are the exact answer to the Giants' most critical needs." Yet not even Stoneham, in this grandiose apology to Minneapolis fans who had fallen in love with the young center fielder, really knew how right he was.

Mays is the first player since DiMaggio to live up to—nay, live beyond—his build-up. Mays had to because he had no build-up to speak of. Few fans will forget the build-up accorded Mickey Mantle, who came to the Yankees and was back in Kansas City the same year. Or Clint Hartung, who could do anything and wound up doing nothing.

And there is a further complication. Mays, DiMaggio, Mantle, Hartung—all played for New York teams. New York baseball writers are adept at the advance build-up. They are disliked by writers in other towns for this reason. Chicago writers will tell you bitterly that Luke Appling, long of White Sox fame, would be an all-time great if he had played for a New York team. There is some foundation for their bitterness.

But the result of such bitterness is that frequently it is taken out on the player, instead of the people who built him up. When Mays appeared in Cleveland for the All-Star Game in 1954, he stood in center field, and alongside him on the ground was some shiny object which glistened in the sunlight. Peering from the press box, a St. Louis writer murmured, "Look there—Willie's halo just fell off."

The anti-New York feeling among out-of-town baseball writers is a factor larger than many people care to suspect. It has dictated the choice of the most valuable player in one or both leagues, an honor decided by the votes of three writers in each of the eight cities in the league. It has even led ball clubs, who are more cognizant of their local writers than either they or the writers would care to admit, to come "up" for a series with a New York team.

Thus it was an honor of signal proportions for Mays to be chosen Most Valuable Player in the National League in the winter of 1954-55 following his first full season in the majors. Not only did he overcome the anti–New York sentiment among the writers, minimal though that had to be in a year when the Giants and Dodgers finished one–two, but he won despite the fact that, among the top five vote-getters, four played for New York teams—three for the Giants and one for Brooklyn. That meant that there was likely a good deal of vote-splitting, even among the New York writers. Yet Willie won big, placing first on sixteen of the twenty-four ballots and, under the point system, coming in with a spread of 66 over the runner-up, 283 to 217 for Ted Kluszewski of Cincinnati.

In a bigger sense, Mays captured the Sporting News Award as Major League Player of the year. In an even bigger one, he won the Associated Press poll to determine the "male athlete of the year." The year 1954 was, after all, the year that man finally ran the four-minute mile. And yet Roger Bannister, who beat John Landy at the British

INTRODUCTION

Empire Games in the "miracle mile" where both runners were clocked under four minutes, had to settle for second place to Mays in the AP poll.

Certainly Mays won his 1954 National League batting championship the hard way. On the last day of the season he got a single, a double, and a triple off the best pitcher in baseball, Robin Roberts of Philadelphia. Mays was at a further disadvantage in his final-day quest. He was a right-handed hitter against a right-handed pitcher. His team-mate Don Mueller, and Duke Snider of Brooklyn, both led Mays in the averages going into their final games. Both were left-handed hitters going against right-handed pitchers, Mueller against Roberts and Snider against Jake Thies of Pittsburgh. The percentage was with Mueller and Snider. Such are percentages. Such is Willie Mays.

Certainly the New York Giants have felt their eggshell way with this amazing young center fielder. They have supplied him with chaperons, and managers, and agents, and more managers and more agents. Willie himself does not particularly like the regulated life he has found himself leading. But, in wishing it might be otherwise, he takes the realistic view. It can safely be said that success, attention, and publicity have had little bad effect upon him—proof positive of this is his enduring and genuine popularity with his teammates, who treat him with rough adoration. And he joins them in taking a somewhat jaundiced view of the legends that have grown up around him . . . among them the hardy myth that his vocabulary consists of only two words: "Say, hey."

What Mays has to say for himself is largely a point of view, and that point of view mostly concerns baseball.

WHY WILLIE?

It is his living and what he likes best to do, and that is the purpose of this book—that, and the thought that, for all the millions of words that already have been written about him, it is high time somebody heard from Willie.

—CHARLES EINSTEIN

BORN TO PLAY BALL

Chapter 1

THE MAYS YOU DON'T SEE

THE way to meet me is to meet the other Willie Mays first, because that way you get to know who I'm not.

Late in the 1954 baseball season, there was a story in a sports magazine, and the title of it was, "Is There a Willie Mays?" Along about that time, I was asking myself the same thing.

I finally decided there must be two of us.

First, shake hands with the other Willie Mays. He's Captain Video or somebody. Boy, what he can do! He socks home runs in his sleep, even off Robin Roberts, and he can hit for seven sewers in stickball. If a fly ball is 40 feet over his head, then that's okay, don't you worry about it, because The Amazing Mays is going to climb up the wall perpendicular and make the catch. And throw? Man, when he was two years old he could throw a baseball a quarter-mile on the fly.

This other Willie Mays, he sleeps with a box of baseballs for a pillow and picks his teeth with a bat. He's either the greatest or the most.

3

And brother, nobody ever had to teach him a thing.

I want to tell you one thing—this guy who's got the same name as mine is all right.

You got to admire him.

I only wish it was me.

Me? It's not hard to get to know me. I mean me myself, not the other Willie. Like I say, it's not hard. Some guys make it hard on themselves. I can remember what it was like just trying to get dressed for a ball game during the '54 season. Seemed like every day there'd be somebody waiting for me in front of my locker with a notebook and a pencil in his hand. He'd get up to shake hands and he'd say, "Willie, my name is Mumble from the *Daily Jumble*." I'd open my mouth to say Hello and he'd say, "Now, before we begin I want to tell you something. Act natural."

Well, I laugh easy, and things like that make me laugh.

"I'm serious," this Mr. Mumble would say. "I want to capture the true Willie Mays. The real you."

Well, you gotta laugh. You laugh, and Mr. Mumble from the *Daily Jumble* takes notes on the way you laugh. Then he says to you, "Don't get nervous. Pretend I'm not here."

I say, "It's hard to make out you're not here when you're sitting so I can't get to my locker to get dressed."

He takes more notes.

Right then and there, who comes over but Leo Durocher, the Skip. He's got a scowl on his face half a mile deep. He points a finger at me and says, "You!"

Boy, this guy Mumble from the *Daily Jumble* jumps like to die. *This* he's got to get. This is the inside stuff.

"You," Durocher says to me, talking like a D.A. or

something. "I know where you were last night. What do you think of that?"

The truth is, I wasn't anyplace last night, but I'm not going to tell Leo that. So I say, "You don't know."

"Oh, yes I do," the Skip says.

"No, you don't," I say. "Isn't any way you could find out."

"I found out," Leo says in that big voice of his. "You know who told me?"

Henry Thompson, whose locker is alongside mine back in the corner of the clubhouse, looks up and says, "Who?"

"Roosevelt, that's who," Durocher says. Roosevelt is the name of a guy we know. He buddies around with us sometimes.

But Henry says, "Roosevelt? Never heard of him."

"You heard of him all right," the Skip says.

"Oh," Henry says, "you mean F.D.R."

That's the way it goes in the clubhouse with the New York Giants. But this fellow Mr. Mumble from the *Daily Jumble*, he doesn't know that. He's the most confused guy you ever saw. By the time he gets around to asking me some questions, he can't think of anything to ask except something like "Tell me confidentially, Willie, who's the worst pitcher you got?"

I wish I knew where they get some of those questions. After the last game of the '54 season, the Giants went on a coast-to-coast television show. We'd beat Roberts in extra innings at Philadelphia, and Don Mueller and I had started the day just about tied for the league hitting lead, along with Duke Snider of Brooklyn. Close was no word

5

for it. Don was at .3426, Snider at .3425, and I was .3422. Boy, they wouldn't let you in the ball park that final day unless you got a slide rule with you. All of a sudden, everybody you met was a certified public accountant.

Snider couldn't get a hit off of Jake Thies of Pittsburgh in his last game, but Don and I both hit Roberts. I got three hits and Don got two and a near miss, and that night this guy on this nationwide television show said to me right in front of everybody, "How does it feel beating out your teammate Don Mueller for the batting title?"

If you've got a smart answer to that, I'll buy it. What I did was to mutter something about if the hits had gone the other way, then Don would've beat me, and if it hadn't been me I would have liked it to be him. Something like that. I felt like hollering, "Roomie! Come over here and take care of this man!"

Roomie—that's Monte Irvin. He and I room together when the ball club's on the road. Many's the time I've hollered for him to get me out of what I'm in. Like the time we were posing for the team picture and a guy came up to me and said, "Willie, I'm Jumble from the *Daily Mumble*," and wanted me to predict the outcome of the world series. I told him that was writers' business like him, making predictions. I wasn't any good at making predictions. The only prediction I can remember making was late in 1954 when I said I wasn't going to win the hitting title.

"Well," Mr. Jumble from the *Daily Mumble* said, "haven't you got any idea how the series is going to go?"

"Yes," I said. "I got an idea. First two games be played at the Polo Grounds. Then we go to Cleveland."

6

"Listen," Jumble said, "I'm not asking these questions for fun. Asking questions is my business."

"I got a business too," I said. "Playing outfield."

"All right," he said, "then how would you compare your outfield with theirs?"

"Roomie!" I yelled out. "Come over here and take care of this man!"

Later on, I saw Irvin on the field. He said, "Who was that guy you put on to me?"

"I don't know," I said. "Did you answer his questions?"

"He only asked me one question," Monte said. "Only question he asked me was could I get him some world series tickets."

But I wasn't fooling. I wasn't fooling when I told this man that baseball is my business. On a television show one time I was asked, "Willie, is it true you'd play ball for nothing?"

"Well," I answered, "that's how every ballplayer gets his start."

Baseball *is* a business—but it's like everything else. If you like the business you're in, you're bound to do better. There was a pitcher for the Chicago Cubs one time, and he was sitting on the bench watching fielding practice before the opening game of the year. A newspaperman came over to him and said, "How you feel?"

"I wish the season was over," the pitcher said.

There are ballplayers like that—none of them on the New York Giants, though. That's one thing a man named Durocher won't put up with. You'll be sitting on the bench not doing much of anything, maybe, and all of a sudden he'll point that finger at you and yell, "What kind of pitch was that?" And you'd better *know*.

You want to win, you're a better ballplayer. You play for a *club* that wants to win, you're a better ballplayer yet. Late in the 1954 season, Joe Garagiola, who'd caught for three other National League teams, came to the Giants. About a week after that, he told me, "You know something? All season long, watching you guys while I was with another club, I had the feeling, *This is luck ... this ball club isn't as good as the papers make out ... these Giants are just another team, only lucky so far, is all.*" Then Joe added: "But you can believe this or not—I come to the Giants and I'm with the club for a day, maybe two days, and all of a sudden I knew different. I realized they won because they were bound to win. I've never seen anything like it in baseball before."

One of the things he hadn't seen in baseball before was something that you have to feel to believe. I want to tell you there is nothing in the world that compares with the Giant fans. Giant fans are ... well, there's no describing them, except that they're different than any other fans in baseball. They're the most wonderful.

One of the things about the Giant fan is he's just about the only fan in the game who'd just as soon see his team in the field as at bat. The Giant fan loves defense. The Polo Grounds is tailor-made for him because it's a defensive ball park. It really is. I know you've all read about the home-run distances down the foul lines at our park and about the gags that have grown up around them, like the one I heard last year about a center fielder in another ball park who started to chase a long fly ball. He could

8

see it was going out of the park, but he saw also that the exit gate was open in center field. So he ran right through the gate and kept going, up a long street leading away from the ball park. There was a fire engine going by, sixty miles an hour, so this center fielder jumped on the fire engine, and nine blocks farther on he caught up with the ball, stuck his glove up in the air, and made the catch.

Well, there were two firemen riding on the back of the truck. One turned to the other and said, "You know something? That would have been a home run at the Polo Grounds."

But let me tell you something, that Polo Grounds is not a home-run paradise—not, maybe, so much because you can't hit homers there as because it takes so much pitching and defense to win. Proof? Sure, there's proof. Look at the New York Giants of 1947. As a team, they hit 221 home runs—an all-time major league record. But they didn't finish anywheres near the pennant.

Actually, the walls at the Polo Grounds drop away from those short foul lines so fast and so far that anything besides a straight pull down the line has got to be the real long ball, or it won't go in. There were half a dozen ter-rific shots in the first two games of the 1954 world series that were all caught by outfielders—but would have been homers if we'd been playing in Cleveland's ball park in-stead of our own. And don't think that gave the Giants any kind of edge—some of those drives were hit by our own men: Al Dark, for instance, who sent Smith of Cleveland practically to the far-away bull pen in left field with a tremendous shot. And all it was was a fly ball out.

The Giant fans know all about this. After all, most hits

9

in baseball come in the general center field area. That is, if you're standing at home plate and you draw a line running out just to the right of where the second baseman usually plays, and another line going just to the left of where the shortstop usually plays, you'll find the area in between takes in the most square footage on the field. (By the way, that's what they had in mind when they thought up the old baseball saying, "Strong down the middle." The team that's strong down the middle is a team to watch because its strength is where the most important area of the field is.)

And I can tell you firsthand, there's no center field like the center field at the Polo Grounds. From home plate to the bleacher wall, it's 460 feet. And just as much to the left and right corners. And there's an indentation in between the two sets of bleachers, where the locker rooms are, so if you hit it to dead center, it's nearly 500 feet into that slot there before you come to anything that's going to stop the ball—or stop you from getting to it.

Luke Easter hit one into the bleachers at the Polo Grounds some time ago, when he was playing Negro ball, and Joe Adcock hit one, but I don't think anybody else ever did. I've hit a couple to the base of the bleacher wall. I've hit one that went even farther than that, which I'll tell you about later when we get to talking about how it was in the '54 season.

Right here we're talking about Giant fans. They love to see that defense. You talk to them about Bill Terry, and they'll tell you all about the beautiful way he could play first base—even though Terry is the last man in the history of the National League to hit over .400. But no.

THE MAYS YOU DON'T SEE

All the Giant fans want to talk about is Terry's fielding. They come out to the ball park to watch the pitching. A Giant fan says to you, "Man, I'm coming out there today. Gotta see that Antonelli pitch." Or Maglie or Ruben Gomez, or like it used to be, Hubbell and Schumacher and Fitzsimmons and Melton and Harry Gumbert on those great Giant teams of the mid-1930's, when I was five years old back in Fairfield, Alabama. Or Christy Mathewson 'way back when.

You get the idea that the Giant fan is a guy with a whole lot of hope and maybe not too much else, and that's all right. The real Giant fan doesn't get the idea that he could have hit a ball that you didn't hit, like the fans do other places. The Giant fan just hopes along with you. Like as not, he doesn't make too much noise about it, either. I can remember what the noise from the stands was like in the second and third play-off games against the Dodgers in 1951. The first game of the play-off, which we won, was played at Ebbets Field. Then we came to the Polo Grounds for the next two.

We lost the second game to Clem Labine and the Dodgers, lost it bad, so that put everything riding on that third game, and we were trailing in that one by 4 to 1 going into the last of the ninth.

That was the game we won 5 to 4 on Bobby Thomson's ninth-inning homer. The point I'm making about it here is that in that second game of the play-off, and right up to and including Thomson's "miracle" homer in the third game, you would have sworn from the crowd noises that we were playing the games in Brooklyn, not at the Polo Grounds.

BORN TO PLAY BALL

It wasn't that there weren't any Giant fans around. It was just that they were being quiet. They weren't razzing us like the fans do when their teams are going bad in other cities around the league. They were just sitting there and hurting and hoping. You get to know the Giant fan. He loves you. You love him. Cab drivers hit him in the middle of the street, busses don't wait for him, subway crowds push him off at the wrong station, his boss yells at him, his wife leaves home, his kids get blamed for hitting the teacher with the spitball in school, he's got doctor bills he worries about so bad he winds up with more doctor bills for an ulcer...

... but he's got the Giants. He doesn't say much about them. Like as not you can tell a Dodger fan or a Yankee fan just from looking at them. The Dodger fan walks around in his undershirt with a handkerchief tied around his forehead and a tuba under his arm. The Yankee fan drives up in a Cadillac. The Giant fan, like as not, is known only to another Giant fan. Maybe they got a password. Maybe they can just look at each other and tell.

It's something private with them. In July of '54 we beat the Dodgers six straight, but the Giant fans kept pretty quiet about it. When you're hoping, you keep your mouth shut. Imagine what kind of place New York would've been to live in if it had been the Dodgers winning those six straight from us. You'd've had to leave town.

Life is maybe just one long ninth inning for the Giant fan. He never leaves the ball park till the last man's out ... no getting away early to beat the crowd for him. And let me tell you something—I know just how it feels. For a while there in '54 it seemed like life was all late innings for us Giants, too.

No, they don't make much noise about it, but if you ask me, New York is a Giant town. The New York Yankees won their pennant in 1949 and again in 1950 and again in 1951 and again in 1952 and again in 1953. And took the world series each time. And were congratulated for it, and that was all.

But the Giants—they win the pennant in '54, clinching a week early, first place most of the season long—and what happened? Next thing we knew we were riding up Broadway in a ticker-tape parade that the cops said was as big as Lindbergh and MacArthur! There was more than a million people cheering at us! I'll never forget it as long as I live.

They like their baseball, those Giant fans, and maybe one of the big reasons is that it's a game where nothing's decided till the last man makes out. You think about that for a minute. How many sports can you think of where that's true? Tennis, is the only one I can think of. Everything else, you've got a clock on you, like in football and basketball, or distance against you, like in a track meet where you've got to make up too many yards in too little remaining time; or, in golf, maybe you come to the eighteenth hole needing a hole-in-one on a par five to win, and you know you can't do it. Even boxing. I've seen a man win on points while he was lying on the floor because the last bell saved him from a knockout.

But not baseball. In baseball, it's up to you. That's one of the things I like most about it. Nobody made a mistake calling it the Great American Game.

BORN TO PLAY BALL

I like grandstands full of people and the flags up on top of the roof of the stands, and I like the feeling you get running out to the field for the first inning and the fans yelling for you. I like the feel of the long hit in the bat. That other Willie Mays we were talking about back at the beginning, I don't know how he feels about this kind of thing. He probably figures he's got it coming.

Not this Willie Mays right here. Nothing's coming to you in baseball. You work for what you get. Sometimes you wonder. You're not Superman. Up to now, I've never seen anybody bother to tell the story of how I came up to the Giants from Minneapolis in 1951, but here's the truth of it: I didn't want to come. I told Tommy Heath, the Minneapolis manager, to tell Leo I wasn't coming. I just wasn't sure I could make it in the big league.

That's the Mays you don't see, the one I'm talking about now. The same one I'll be talking about right through this book. If you're looking for Captain Marvel or somebody, you're in the wrong ball park. Let's face up to it. The biggest kick I ever got from a home run came on a home run I didn't hit. Somebody else hit it. The fielding play that brought me the biggest wallop was a routine fly ball that somebody else caught.

I'm supposed to be the life of the clubhouse, but when it came to celebrating those magic pennant victories in 1951 and 1954, I was the saddest sack you ever laid eyes on. They poured me a glass of champagne after that dramatic '51 clincher—I was just past twenty years old at the time— and I said to Henry Thompson, "What's this?"

"Champagne," Henry said.

"How do you drink it?" I said.

14

"Like an egg cream," Henry said, and grinned.

So I drank it down and passed out. Sicker than a dog.

Around rolled 1954, and I was grown up by now. Twenty-three years old. We clinched against the Dodgers in a night game, and there was the champagne, all ready and waiting, in the clubhouse.

Next day, Thompson said to me, "Congratulations."

"What for?" I said.

"Remember that last pennant?" he said. "You had a glass of champagne and you were on the floor."

"So what?" I said. "I was on the floor again last night, too."

"I know," Henry said, "but this time it took two glasses."

Chapter 2

THE PLAYS YOU DON'T SEE

FOR a while there, in the 1954 season, I had a funny feeling. It was this: You couldn't pick up a sports page hardly, without reading where some new guy was taking credit for the fact that he never taught me anything.

It seemed to be some kind of badge or something. Everybody had to go around and shake the hand of the man who didn't teach Willie Mays anything.

It was not only a funny feeling to have—it was something that couldn't have been less true.

I don't think there's another business where you can get to a point where you've learned things you never even dreamed about—and yet have most of your learning yet to come.

You figure a minor leaguer coming up to the majors knows pretty much what there is to know about baseball. It just doesn't fall that way.

I can remember the third or fourth game I was with the Giants. I had come down the clubhouse steps at the Polo Grounds and was on my way in to the bench for the start

of batting practice before a game when I heard a voice behind me.

"Hey, Hubbell!"

I turned around. It was Leo Durocher.

I said, "What'd you call me?"

"Hubbell," the Skip said.

"Carl Hubbell?"

"That's right."

"What for?"

"Because of the way you wear your pants," Durocher
said. And it was true. I had the habit of wearing my baseball pants long and low, the legs going down well past
the knees, the way Hubbell wore his.

Well, I laughed a little and started walking to the dugout again. But again I heard Leo's voice behind me.

"Hey, Hubbell."

"What now?" I said.

"Pull the pants higher. Get the legs up."

"What for?" I said.

"Shorten your strike zone," Leo said.

And he was right, of course. The strike zone is between
the shoulder and the knee. A guy who wears his pants so
low you can't tell where the knees are may find an umpire
calling a strike on a low pitch.

But would *you* have thought of something like that?

How many other things did I learn? There's just no
counting them. I learned an awful lot about a thing called
inside baseball. I learned, for one thing, that in baseball
sometimes the big play of the game is the play you never
see.

Sometimes you do see them, but don't pay them any

17

mind. Other times you figure them out wrong and don't get what the team was really trying to do.

Sometimes you just plain don't see them at all.

You'd be surprised—as I was—not only at the amount of inside stuff that goes on, but how much time ball clubs in the big leagues spend working on those kinds of plays.

A story fits in here—one about how old Casey Stengel worked for weeks figuring out a new pick-off play on a runner at third base. That was in the days when Casey had the Boston Bees in the National League, and Stengel had it figured where his pitcher would throw the ball real close to the hitter and yell out a warning at the same time. The hitter would jump out of the way and the catcher would whip the ball down to third. Casey had it doped out where with all that going on—the pitcher screaming and the hitter jumping out of the way and everything—why, that man leading off third base would just freeze there in his tracks and forget to dive back when the throw came.

Well, finally they tried it in a game and it worked fine— except for one thing. That man leading off third froze in his tracks, all right, just as Casey had planned.

But Casey's third baseman froze worse. The throw from the catcher went right by him and into left field.

There's a point to be made by that story—a good point, I think. And it's this: Like on that play of Stengel's, about the only time you come to notice the inside stuff is when it doesn't work.

In the 1954 season, there was a play in a game between the Dodgers and the Phillies where the Phillies were ahead 2 to 1 in the second inning and had Richie Ashburn on first base with one out. The next man hit a short, high looper along the left-field line. Walt Moryn, playing left for the Dodgers, was the only man with a shot at it. He came tearing over on the long run, just did get the ball one-handed, and threw it back to first base. It was the easiest double play you ever saw. Ashburn was around third base by the time the ball was caught.

Next day, one of the papers writing about the game said Ashburn ran all out because "he apparently thought the ball would not be caught." Another paper said "he seemed to think there were two out at the time."

Now I don't live inside Richie Ashburn's head, but I'll stand the Cokes that both those write-ups had it wrong.

Let's say you're a fast man like Ashburn, and you're in the same situation—a run or so ahead in an early inning, leading off first base with one out—and your batter hits that same kind of looper.

If it's just a question of reasonable doubt as to whether the ball will be caught or not, you don't necessarily just put your head down and run.

But if there's that doubt—plus the fact that the ball will stay up there long enough for you to *score* ahead of a play if it's not caught—then sure you run. You got the house odds going for you. You're not assuming it's going to fall safely—you're not assuming there are two out when it's only one out.

You're just plain taking a good gamble on scoring a run.

If the ball won't stay up long enough for you to get home, then it's not worth the risk because you could get to second base anyway by playing it safe and sticking close to first. But if it's going to hang up there, then take the gamble and go.

19

The point is, the thing with Ashburn was a definite play that's used time and again in baseball. People don't realize it for what it is because the kind of situation that calls for it doesn't come along every day—and also because more times than not, *it works!* And then what do the papers say? "Heads-up base-running enabled So-and-So to score all the way from first." (!) But if he doesn't make it, the idiot thought there was two out.

I learned something else nobody seems to think of... something about cut-off plays. The cut-off play in baseball is one of the most beautiful of all to watch. Basically, what it is comes down to this: With at least two runners in motion, an infielder stations himself in a direct line with the outfielder's throw to a base. The infielder has the option of letting the throw ride through or cutting it off and throwing it to another base to get another runner. In practice, the cut-off, nine times out of ten, involves a throw to the *farthest* base—either in terms of a runner's advance (a man trying for home from first on a double; trying for home from second on a single; trying for third from first on a single), or in terms of the *distance* of the outfielder's throw (third base on a single to right field, for instance). In other words, the play almost always starts out as a play on a more advanced runner; if cut off, the ball will be thrown to a base to get a succeeding runner. In terms of the distance an outfielder has to throw, you can occasionally get a cut-off play without a cut-off man. For instance, with a man on first and a single to left or left-center, the throw may go through to third without a cut-off man in-between the outfielder and the third baseman.

Then the third baseman serves as his own cut-off man to throw the ball to second in case the hitter tries for the extra base. The factor there would be the fact that the outfielder's throw to third is relatively short.

Complicated? Sure. And yet I had all of that pretty much in mind when I came up to the big league—or so I thought.

Then one day I was talking to someone—I think it was Monte Irvin, our left fielder—about throws from the outfield. There's been a lot said and written about the way I throw. Tris Speaker is supposed to have met me in Dallas during spring training in 1954, and he's supposed to have told me I was throwing too high—throwing balls that couldn't be cut off, in other words. And the story is that as a result of his advice, I lowered my throws to the point where Durocher had to tell me to get them up again.

A nice story, but I never even met Speaker till before the third game of the '54 world series, where they posed us together at Municipal Stadium in Cleveland.

No, this conversation with Irvin took place three years before that. He said to me, "Ever notice how that cut-off man stands in a straight line between you and where you're throwing?"

"Sure," I said. "Where else would he stand?"

Monte shook his head. "The point is," he said, "he's made to order for your throw. *Aim on him!* Then if he wants to cut it off, he's got it. If he wants to let it ride through, the catcher's got it. Or the third baseman."

I said, "What's wrong with aiming on the catcher to begin with?"

"Nothing," Monte said. "Except you're taking target

practice with a .22. Which would you rather have? A close target or a far target?"

"Close," I said.

"There's your answer," he said.

The result of that has been some throws that otherwise I wouldn't have made. When I made my throw on Billy Cox of Brooklyn in 1951, a throw they still talk about, I came out of a turn and saw Whitey Lockman and threw at him. Lockman was the cut-off man. He just stepped to one side, let the ball ride through to the plate, and we had Cox.

Speaking of outfielders' throws, it may have been that a bad throw, made by one of our own men, was a big help to us in the '54 world series against Cleveland. I say "may have been" because this is more or less a second guess, and you can't second-guess baseball. Of course, everybody does it. It's a big indoor sport. Maybe Roy Campanella puts it better. He says, "In baseball, you can't second-guess a winner."

But here's the story: In the opening game of the world series, Don Mueller threw *behind* a runner—a man who'd singled. Don threw the ball back to first base after the runner had made his turn. The throw was a fraction too high for Lockman, and the runner got to second.

Now, after the world series was over, all the papers made a lot of the fact that Cleveland had played conservative baseball (only "conservative" wasn't the word some of the papers used). Throwing behind a runner isn't a conservative play. Maybe—I say, just maybe—the Indians saw Don make that behind-the-runner play unsuccessfully.

If he'd done it successfully, maybe—I say maybe—they might have got the idea to try it, too.

But the way it fell, they didn't throw behind a runner of ours all series long. All Don Mueller's got to show for it is an error in the record book. Maybe he should have a medal instead.

Don't think for a minute that this kind of thing doesn't mean much in a big series. I'll never forget the account of how Joe DiMaggio scared a world series opponent with a sore arm. And if you can do that, you're all right!

DiMaggio and the Yankees played the Brooklyn Dodgers in the 1947 world series. DiMag's arm, to hear his account, was killing him every time he made a throw.

But on each day of that world series, he made two magnificent throws—one to the plate, another to third base—*in fielding practice!*

It near killed him to do it.

But he knew the Dodgers were watching.

And they didn't run on his arm all series. They could have, but they didn't. They'd seen the throws he made in practice.

From time to time in a ball game, the crowd sees exactly what's happening, but reads it all wrong. For instance, in a big night game against the Dodgers in September of '54, the score was tied in a late inning and we had men on first and third and Hoyt Wilhelm was hitting for us. Matter of fact, he was hitting for himself, which was unusual enough.

It was really a big game, that one—the start of a three-

23

game series between us and the second-place Dodgers, with the Giants leading Brooklyn in the standings by three games. The date: September 3. If you had to pick any "big" game of the season, which is something you can't very well do—but if you had to pick *one*, then you'd have a hard time overlooking this one.

The fans didn't overlook it. We had a house of 46,611.

Anyway, Wilhelm came into the game with the score tied at 4-4, replacing Sal Maglie. Monte Irvin had pinch-hit for Maglie in the bottom of the sixth when we scored twice to tie the score. (Monte got the pinch single, by the way.)

Now, in the last of the seventh, manager Durocher had a decision to make. Don Mueller had walked, and Davey Williams had sent him to third with a simply beautiful hit-and-run single. Davey almost had to throw his bat at the ball, but he punched it through the hole into right field.

Two out, and it was Wilhelm's turn to bat. Leo decided to go with him.

And all of a sudden the Dodgers were grouped around the pitching mound, having the biggest conference you ever saw. Everybody was in there talking except Walter O'Malley, the president of the club.

Well, Wilhelm isn't quite the hitter that he is a pitcher. (As I'll tell later, Hoyt was one of the few pitchers ever to be taken out of a game because he was too good!)

As a hitter, though, Wilhelm had gone 15-for-0 at the plate in all of 1954 up to this particular moment.

So people in the stands naturally assumed that the Dodgers, in their big meeting at the mound, were talking

24

over the way they'd play it if the Giants, with two fine
base runners, Mueller and Williams, already on, took the
logical two-out gamble for the run with the hitless Wilhelm at bat.

That logical gamble would have been that wing-ding of
all baseball plays—the double steal.

Sure, the Dodgers did talk about that. But they had been
in the double-steal jackpot before. Theirs was a good
defensive infield (Reese at short, Gilliam at second—what
more could you ask?).

No, the main thing they were talking about in that big
revival meeting at the pitcher's mound was just plain this:
How do you pitch to Hoyt Wilhelm?

None of them had ever seen him hit before!

And don't think it was ridiculous, staging a meeting like
that in the middle of the diamond to talk over how to pitch
to a .ooo hitter. The Dodgers didn't think it was ridiculous.

They had only one thing to go by—the old axiom, never
pitch high to a pitcher.

So they didn't pitch him high.

They still don't think it was ridiculous, by the way, that
big conference.

Why?

Because Wilhelm singled to center to beat them.

Those conferences in the middle of the infield intrigue a
lot of fans. (You know the old saying, "What does the
catcher tell the pitcher?")

It would have been great to listen in on some of the
dialogues between Lefty Gomez and his catcher, Bill

25

Dickey. Nobody ever talked Gomez down. One time somebody asked him, "As a pitcher, what do you consider your greatest asset?" And Lefty replied, "Fast outfielders."

Once Gomez shook Dickey off time and again, until finally the catcher ran out to the mound. The great Jimmy Foxx was the hitter, and Dickey said to Gomez, "All right. I signaled for the fast ball and you said No, so I switched to the curve and you said No, so I switched to the change-up and you said No. So you tell me. What do you want to throw him?"

"I don't want to throw the ball at all," Gomez said.

Another story that I've heard fits in here—about a rookie pitcher for Brooklyn who called Jacques Fournier over from first base to ask him how he was supposed to pitch to Rogers Hornsby.

"Low and inside," Fournier said, and went back to first base.

The rookie pitched low and inside to Hornsby who, as a right-handed batter, promptly tripled down the left-field line.

The bush pitcher called Fournier over. "I thought you said low and inside."

"I did," Fournier said.

"That didn't get him out," the pitcher said.

"I didn't say it would get him out," Fournier said. "You asked me how to pitch to him, that's all. I've got a wife and family. You think I want him hitting it at me?"

At times a pitcher who shakes off a catcher is doing it only for effect. They've already agreed on the pitch; the pitcher shakes his head to throw the opposition off—to have them trying to steal catcher's signs that don't mean a thing.

And—here's another thing I've learned—you have to watch for things like that when you're playing center field. You not only play for where the hitter is most likely to hit—you play where the hitter is most likely to hit that particular pitch!

Sometimes, by the way, the conference at the pitcher's mound has no other purpose than to give a relief pitcher more time to get ready. There's the classic story about the manager whose pitcher was being racked up in the first inning. It was a big game, and the umpires weren't sitting still for any delays.

The manager strolled out to the mound. After a time, the plate umpire came out. "You want a new pitcher?" he asked.

The manager knew his relief man in the bull pen wasn't ready. "No," he said to the umpire, "but did you get that telegram I sent you?"

"What telegram?" the umpire said.

The manager clapped his hand to his head. "Oh," he said, "maybe I sent it to him instead of you. Ask him." And he pointed at the first-base umpire.

By the time all four umpires had found out that nobody got a telegram from anybody, the relief man was ready.

And at times the conference at the mound is for no other reason than to relieve tension. In the 1946 world series, manager Joe Cronin of the Boston Red Sox went out to the mound to talk to his pitcher, Earl Johnson, in a rough situation in the tenth inning of the first game. The Cardinals, trailing by a run, had a man on third with two out and Enos Slaughter at bat.

Cronin said to Johnson, who was a twice-decorated World War II hero, "Earl, what was the name of that battle you were in?"

Johnson said, "The Battle of the Bulge."

"Well, this isn't it," Cronin said, and went back to the dugout.

Johnson got Slaughter to fly to right field for the game-ending out.

Another delusion that gets ahold of fans from time to time is the purpose of an argument with the umpire. Spectators watching the 1954 All-Star Game at Cleveland —my first All-Star Game, by the way—couldn't figure out why Leo Durocher, who was coaching for the National League at third base, and Charley Grimm, who was coaching back of first, raised such a ruckus with plate umpire Bill Stewart when Red Schoendienst was out trying to steal home. Schoendienst had been clearly tagged out at the plate.

The fact of the matter was, though, that Schoendienst hadn't been sent home from third because Durocher thought he could beat the throw. Instead, what Durocher figured was that the unexpected maneuver might well cause the American League's pitcher, rookie Dean Stone of the Washington Senators, to commit a balk. So it wasn't a question of out or safe on the steal at all.

Maybe the big plays that the fans never notice will get into the box score—and maybe not. One of the best fielding plays in baseball, the ability to hold a man on second close to the bag, never shows up in the record book.

28

But it can win ball games.

The sight of a second baseman or a shortstop scuffing dirt in the direction of a base runner may seem to the casual fan to be nothing more than a mild case of showboating.

But the fact is, anybody can hold a runner close to a base. The trick is to do it at the least sacrifice to the fielding pattern that has to defend against the batted ball.

I remember one game in 1954 when Alvin Dark, who as Giant shortstop is one of the greats at his position in the game today, faked a break toward second base just as our pitcher was about to deliver the ball to the plate. Dark's action at shortstop had the base runner leaning back toward second as the pitch was thrown.

The batter hit the pitch for a single, but the runner on second could make it only to third because Dark had him moving the wrong way—backwards, not forwards, on the pitch!

We got out of the inning and won the ball game by one run.

Another thing that the fan often sees wrong is the actions of the coaches at first and third. Our third-base coach on the Giants took a going-over for waving me home in a big pennant-race game in September of '54. That was the game against the Cardinals where I set the new record for extra-base hits by a Giant in one season. I had doubled in the first inning, and Dusty Rhodes—what a man *he* is!—singled me home. So we led 1 to 0 with Johnny Antonelli going great for us and the Cards's rookie righthander, Gordon Jones, going fine for them.

29

I got a single in the third inning, and Don Mueller smacked a good hit to left-center field, and it would have taken a perfect fielding play and relay to get me at home. The Cards made the play, and I was out on a close call at the plate. Sure you go for the run in a situation like that. And Antonelli took the game anyway, 1 to 0. But just the same, the papers thought I shouldn't have been waved around third.

Sometimes the situation means everything. It doesn't even have to be the situation in the game itself. It can be the team standings, like last year when Al Lopez, managing the Cleveland Indians, let Dave Philley hit away at a 3-and-0 pitch in a big game against the Yankees. The Indians were ahead 2 to 1 in the eighth inning—Early Wynn had allowed only one hit, a home run—and Cleveland had two men on. Philley hit the cripple for the home run and Cleveland won it big. It was a good gamble for Lopez because his club went into that ball game leading the Yanks by 4½ games in the standings—and that was the way to break their backs.

There has been a good deal of speculation as to how much control Leo Durocher exercises from the bench on the way we Giants hit—me especially.

Again, this is something that depends on the situation. Sometimes I've got the green light without even looking, like the time I batted against Ray Crone of the Braves in the last of the eighth inning, last time we played them in September of '54.

We had all but wound up the pennant by then. We'd won the first game of that day's double-header from the Braves, and we were winning the second 5 to 2, and news was already in that Brooklyn had lost its game to Cincinnati.

I was free to swing. I swung like I hadn't swung for half a season. I got me a home run.

But that's not to say I'm on my own every time I come to bat.

I'm not, because—as I said some time ago and say again now—I'm still learning.

With plenty left to go.

Chapter 3

BUCKDUCK

I SAID back at the start that it seemed like there were two Willie Mayses . . . me and the guy you read about in some of the papers.

Well, check that. There used to be *another* Willie Mays too . . . back home in Fairfield, Alabama, a steel town thirteen miles outside of Birmingham.

This Willie Mays had another name: Joe DiMaggio.

Joe D. was my idol in all of baseball. I had a buddy who lived down the street from me in Fairfield, a kid about my age, and a real good athlete. His name was Charles Willis. There was a neighborhood ball field, too—no Polo Grounds, but a level lot with a diamond marked out on it—one that was used so much by the neighborhood kids that it came to look like a real ball field because all the grass wore away at home plate and at the bases and in the middle of the diamond where the pitcher stood.

Afternoons after school, when we were ten, eleven, twelve years old, Charley Willis and I would be down at this field. I had a couple of gloves from my dad, who was an outfielder too, and we'd throw the ball back and forth, and Charley might get up a fly ball that was over my shoulder, and I'd turn and take it going away, and he'd sing out, "Hey, DiMag!"

"That's me!" I'd yell back. "Catch 'em like that all the time!"

The summer I was ten years old, DiMaggio hit in his record fifty-six straight games with the Yankees. With me it felt like every time he came up to bat, I'd be coming up to bat with him.

If it'd been another time when I was born and growing up, I probably would have had somebody else for an idol. But maybe I wouldn't have felt so close about it, because DiMaggio was a center fielder—the position I've always played—and he hit right-handed.

And the fact of it is, my batting stance, right down to today, is a copy of Joe DiMaggio's. I modeled my stance after his, up to a point... and then I had to get practical about it. One of the big things about your stance is the spread between your front and back foot. And your height and weight have an awful lot to do with that.

DiMag is taller than I grew to be, and he weighs more, and so he could plant his feet farther apart. Another thing —if you watch hitters carefully in the big leagues, you'll find that their hitting stance changes from time to time right during the course of a season. It won't change by too much, but it'll change enough so you can notice it if you're looking for it. Changing your stance just a little every once in a while helps keep your batting average up for you—or at least, it doesn't help pitchers keep it down, because every change you make gives a pitcher that much more guesswork.

Essentially, though, I've always had one stance—well-spread, body on a line parallel to the line between the pitcher and the catcher, dug in just enough to get that solid feeling. I don't crowd the plate, but I'm pretty close to it. Many's the pitch I've ducked away from that got the called strike. Many's the pitch that didn't, too.

That gets us back to DiMaggio. I only saw him play once. A number of stories about me have said that he was my idol, all right, but that I never saw him play. Don't worry, I saw him play. Played against him in the 1951 world series (the last game of that series was Joe D.'s last game of baseball). He'd been playing ever since 1936, when I was just turned five years old. They said he wasn't the DiMag of old.

That didn't keep him from breaking open the world series against us. We were leading 2 to 1 in games till he connected for a homer in the fourth game. We never led after that.

The following winter, DiMaggio announced his retirement, and he said two things at that time—and I've always remembered what they were. One of them I couldn't agree with less. The other, I couldn't agree with more.

DiMag said, for the first thing, that he had found the thing he disliked the most about baseball was night games. He said he'd found it took two or three years off of his career.

I've been asked my views on night baseball. Here they are—I like it best of all.

BUCKDUCK

Of course, I can see where DiMaggio would take a different view. After all, he was completely used to day games before night ball became the big thing it is now. He was used to eating the same meals at the same time each day, and to not having to catch a train after a night game for a sleeper jump to another city where you'd be playing a day game the next day.

So I can see where it would play hob with him, but it hasn't with me. I prefer night ball for one simple reason—you don't have to worry about the sun or the sky or the background. Late in 1954, in a game against the Cincinnati Reds, I tied Mel Ott's former New York Giant record of eighty-one extra-base hits in one season. I'm glad I went on to break it before the season ended and set a new mark of eighty-seven—not glad so much for the sake of the record itself, but because if we'd wound up tied at eighty-one each, I would have felt awful about it. That eighty-first extra-base hit of mine was just about the cheapest hit I ever got.

We'd had lousy weather in New York (those hurricanes were coming up the coast one after another), but we were in a hot pennant race and this was Cincinnati's last trip in, so they wanted to get the game played if at all possible. Well, it was possible—but the game started a good couple of hours late, and before it was over they had to turn on the lights. Now, you had the combination of lights on in the ball park before it was really dark enough to need them; gray skies, with no kind of background at all; and the false light you get anyway from twilight.

And in the midst of all that, I hit a lazy fly ball straight at Gus Bell, who was playing center field for the Reds.

35

Gus stood there waiting for it—and then just plain lost it against that sky. It dropped right behind him and I was on second base with what had to be scored as a double.

By the way, I don't mind cheap hits. No hitter does, because any hitter will tell you it gives you no better than an even break anyway. Time and time again some guy will make an unexpected play to take a real hit away from you. So it's no more than your due to have a few flukes fall in. Just so it averages out. I just would have hated to wind up tied with somebody like Ott on that fly ball to Bell, that's all.

That was one of the things DiMaggio talked about, the question of night baseball. The other was when somebody asked him, "Do you think a great outfielder is born with a certain instinct for baseball?"

DiMaggio thought about that for a while. Then he said, "Yes, I do. I think there are some players who are born to play ball."

I think he's absolutely right. I think there's something to the idea of "a born athlete." What it is, I don't rightly know. Probably most people can *learn* to be good in most any sport. Very likely, they can *enjoy* a sport without being good at it—sure, they can, the way baseball fans do. But if you've got that instinct, you've got something nobody can ever take away from you. You're going to *be* there when that ball's hit, and there's nobody can ever teach you to do it quite that well.

Maybe I was born to play ball. Maybe I truly was. It's hard to say that without sounding like you're boasting, but it isn't a boast. I've got too much baseball yet to learn, to sit back and say I'm it.

But, for one thing, sports ran in my family. My grandfather on my father's side, Walter Mays, was a pitcher back in Tuscaloosa, Alabama, along around the turn of the century. My dad loved baseball from the very start. His name was William Howard Mays (William Howard Taft was president when he was born). My name, though, is *not* William Howard Mays, Jr. I'm not a junior. My name, my real name, is Willie.

Anyway, there's a story in our family that my grandfather wanted my dad to be a pitcher like him, only my dad said, "Uh-uh."

"Why not?" my grandfather asked him.

"I don't want 'em hitting any home runs off of *me*," Dad is supposed to have answered.

Dad went on to become an outfielder. And one time, when he caught me pitching in a pick-up game, he came over and said, "You know, pitchers don't get to play every day."

I did a little pitching till I was about fourteen years old. That summer, I pitched a whole nine innings for a local team in a sandlot game and hit a home run to wind it up. Going across home plate, I felt my head start spinning. It had been a hot day. And I'd been playing harder than I knew.

"Outfield for you," my dad said after that. And he meant it.

He himself played sandlot and semi-pro ball on a good number of teams. He could probably go out there and give it nine innings today, but he hung up his spikes shortly after I first got into the game for keeps. "One's enough in this family," he told me, laughing.

37

BORN TO PLAY BALL

I was born on May 6, 1931. My dad was just about eighteen at the time. A couple of years after that, he and my mother were divorced. My mother remarried, and I went to live with my aunt Sarah—the wife of my father's brother—in a five-room frame house in Fairfield. I have ten half brothers and sisters by my mother's second marriage, and even though we did not live together, I always found myself "the big brother." It was a dark moment in our lives when my mother died from complications arising from the birth of her eleventh child, Diana, in November of 1953.

I like to think that my mother, whose name was Ann, played a part in my athletic heritage. She had been a wonderful track athlete as a young girl in school.

My aunt Sarah is gone now, too. She passed on in July of 1954. My childhood life in her house was fine and warm. It's been said of my boyhood that I had to go out and pick cotton, or work in the steel mills, or something like that to help keep everybody going. That's not the real story. I'm not old enough to remember the height of the depression. Far back as I can remember, Franklin D. Roosevelt was already in his second term as president. But I don't recall that we had any suffering. As far as I remember, my dad always had work in the steel mills at Fairfield. We didn't have a Cadillac, but neither did the people next door. And there was our own one-family house.

Another thing that started up somewhere in the days back before I remember was my nickname—Buckduck. To this day, folks around home back in Birmingham all call me Buckduck. Why, I'll never know, and there's nobody can tell me. It's just one of those names that come along and get ahold of you and hang on. Everybody calls me Buckduck back home.

There is one big story about when I was just about a year old, and that is that my dad would come home from working at the mills and get out a rubber ball and roll it across the floor at me for hours on end. The way the story goes, I'd sit there and roll it right back at him. See? A year old and I was already playing catch! Don't ask me if it really happened that way or not.

There was one time, though, when my dad passed by the ball field in the neighborhood, and there I was, running the bases like crazy, all by myself!

"Who's that?" my dad asked me.

"DiMaggio," I said.

"Okay, DiMaggio," he said. "Let's get the bat and glove. Kitty Kat's going to show you pepper."

That was Dad's baseball nickname—Kitty Kat.

About the pepper, I didn't know what he meant.

But he showed me. I guess I was about ten at the time. I'd throw the ball at him, standing there with a bat about fifteen feet away, and he'd tap it back at me.

"Pick it up!" he'd yell. "Pick it up!"

Or, "You're dug in like a potato plant! How can you go to the side? Bend those knees!"

Of all the training I have received in baseball, none was more valuable than this. To this day, I'll play pepper by the hour. I'll go out to shortstop between turns in the batting cage before the game, too, to field hot ground balls. Not many outfielders do this. They ought to. In a free-hitting game, you'll get as many balls on the ground as in the air out there in the outfield—maybe more. There'll be

39

all kinds of them—balls on the roll at all kinds of angles after being hit out there on a line, ground hits through the middle, caroms off the walls.

And the purpose of that before-game fielding work isn't just to make you a better fielder, though through the years it'll do that, too. The bigger purpose is to get you accustomed to all kinds of hits, so the first few shots that are hit your way in the actual game don't find you unprepared . . . they're nothing more or less than what you were handling just before the game began.

Growing up around my dad, I got to meet a lot of ballplayers. It was a good home life. Aunt Sarah was there to see that I ate right and behaved myself and went to Sunday school regularly, and there was always baseball. It's a funny thing. In this great big wonderful country of ours, I'd be willing to bet that there's not a single young baseball player anywhere who can't make it into professional ball if he's got the stuff. Don't worry about being overlooked. If you've got the stuff, they'll find you.

Of course, that's even more so of colored baseball, which into my teens was a sort of sport in itself, where anybody either knew or had heard of everybody else. That's still true today, although Negro athletes now play in organized ball, too. And this is a good place for me to point out in passing that by the time I made it into organized ball, the color question was not a personal problem for me. Jackie Robinson had been with Montreal in 1946 and was in the big league with Brooklyn in '47. About the only thing it meant in my case was that I had several ready-made friends, like Monte Irvin on the Giants, whom I'd known already, when I finally came up to the big league.

I was a big kid, once I filled out, along about when I got to be sixteen years of age. I'd never had any major illnesses as a kid—nothing more than all kids get, like colds and chicken pox and measles. But by the time I got to Fairfield Industrial High School, I was a good size. And sports—all sports—were my meat.

I couldn't promise you that baseball was my number one favorite. Our coach at Fairfield, Jim McWilliams, always claimed that football must be the biggest thing with me, because one time when I was thirteen, and still in grade school, I shinnied up a tree to watch Fairfield play West View in football and got so excited I fell out and broke my leg.

McWilliams used me in the backfield in football almost from the start once I got to Fairfield. My arm was a strong one, and I could pass a football for good yardage. But even if I was big for my age, some of those all-senior teams we played were a lot bigger. I got racked up pretty good from time to time. My boyhood friend, Charles Willis, played football on the same team with me, and in one game got hurt so he couldn't play the rest of the season.

If you asked me today whether I like baseball better than football, I'd say baseball—and I think what happened to Charley Willis would be one of the reasons.

I played basketball, too, and I was high scorer in our county the winter I was sixteen.

That was my big year—the winter I was sixteen and when I turned seventeen the following spring. That spring,

41

my dad got ahold of Piper Davis, manager of the Birmingham Barons in the Negro National League.

"He knows about you," my dad said to me. "He'll give you a tryout."

There was a discussion about it. Some of the teachers at school wanted me to plan ahead for college. I'd been taking a special course in cleaning and pressing at school (though the only outside work I'd done was a short stretch of washing dishes in a Birmingham café), and there was the question of having a trade.

My dad said he'd leave it up to me. "Just one thing," he said. "Whatever you do, don't go down to the steel mills to work."

"It's not such bad work," I said.

"No," he said, "but once you're in it, you never get out."

We decided finally to go along with the tryout with the Barons. By the way, I got no money till I'd proved myself. Even so, I knew my high-school athletic eligibility would be over, although I kept up with school through graduation.

I caught on with the Barons (even though manager Davis had to teach me not to overcrowd the plate). "Aim on that pitcher!" Piper would yell. "Don't peek at him!"

My first contract in baseball called for very little money, and Piper said, "I'll up it five bucks a month for every month you're over three hundred." I never did collect a single fin.

Piper tells the story of how I missed the bus one time when we were headed for St. Louis because I'd got caught up in a game of pool. He's got the story right. I've always

42

enjoyed playing pool, and this one night I got so interested I clean missed the bus and had to grab a cab to catch it on its way out of town. "What are you going to leave me here for?" I yelled at Piper when we caught up with the bus. "I'm a pro ballplayer!"

I remember that trip to St. Louis for another reason. We had the Sunday off, and I went out to the ball park there to watch the Browns play the Red Sox. Don't think *that* wasn't a thrill. Not only my first major league ball game, but there was a guy named Ted Williams playing that day. I just sat there with my mouth open, watching the way he cut at the ball.

I got to see a good number of big league parks, traveling with the Barons—including the Polo Grounds in New York. I got to play against and with some pretty fair ballplayers, not only while I was with the Barons, but a year or so later on, when Roy Campanella took me on for his barnstorming team during the winter months. I met Monte Irvin that way, and Henry Thompson, Curt Roberts, and —sure enough—Satchel Paige. I was seventeen the first and only time I came up to hit against the great man. I got one for two off of him.

My days in the Negro National League, and with the barnstormers, led to a couple of funny happenings. One was that we played in Cleveland in the old park the Indians used to use there, League Park—a real bandbox of a place. Next time I played baseball in Cleveland was with the 1954 National League All-Star team—at giant Municipal Stadium, of course. First thing I thought of when I came up the dugout steps was, "Boy, has this place got bigger!"

Another time, when I was playing for Campanella, we were scheduled for a game in New Orleans, and I went up to Campy and said, "There's something I never told you before."

"What's that?" he said.

"I'm not an outfielder," I said, deadpan. "I'm really a shortstop."

"Yeah?" he said.

"Sure," I said. "Start me at short today and see for yourself."

So Campy started me at shortstop. I butchered the first ball that came my way. The second ball that came my way nearly butchered me.

From back of the plate, Campanella threw off his mask and hollered for time. "Change in line-up," he said to the umpire. "The shortstop will now play center field."

Later on Campy said to me, "You get the chair for murder in this state. That's why I got you off of shortstop."

The story of how the Giants scouted me and finally signed me is better left to the people who did it. To this day, I don't know all the details. I do know that it was in 1950, and two Giant scouts, Ed Montague and Bill Harris, came down to Birmingham to take a look at Lou Perry, who was playing first base for the Barons. The Giants wanted a man, I'm told, for delivery to their Class A farm team in Sioux City, Iowa.

Anyway, Montague and Harris came and decided the guy they wanted was me. I found out later the Boston (later Milwaukee) Braves had already made the Barons an offer for my contract, but the Giant offer was better—a flat $10,000, I think it was—and anyway, nobody could do anything, under baseball law, until my high-school class graduated.

Graduation came, and I was Giant property. I never did get to Sioux City, although one night, which I'll tell about in just a little while, I came close.

They started me out in 1950 with Trenton, New Jersey, in the Interstate League. The manager there was Bill McKechnie, Jr., son of the well-known former big-league manager. The first twenty-two times I got up for Trenton, I made out.

I went to McKechnie and said, "How am I going to hit this pitching?"

"Don't worry about it," he said. "You don't strike me as being the worrying kind."

"I'm not," I said.

"Well, don't start in now," he said. "Just go up there and take your swings."

Don't think that was just offhand advice. It meant a lot to me, just as similar advice from Leo Durocher meant in seasons to come.

I did what McKechnie said, and pretty soon I was hitting the ball. In 81 games for Trenton in '50, I hit .353. I had 76 singles, 20 doubles, 8 triples, and 4 homers. I stole 7 bases, knocked in 55 runs, scored 50.

The next season I was promoted to Minneapolis of the American Association—class AAA. Tommy Heath was the manager, and we had our spring training at Sanford, Florida. Just before one night-time exhibition game there, Heath brought a well-dressed athletic-looking man over to say hello to me.

45

"Say, hey!" I said, and shook hands.

"Heard a lot about you," the man said. "Maybe I'll be seeing you around."

"Sure thing," I said.

That was about all there was to my first meeting with Leo Durocher.

I would never have guessed how soon we were going to meet again.

It was late in May, and so far in the 1951 season I'd been going great for Minneapolis. In 35 games, I'd hit 8 home runs and scored 38 runs. My hitting average was 71 for 149, or .477.

In New York, though, the parent Giants weren't happy about things. The New York club had lost its first game of the season, then won its next game, then lost eleven in a row!

We had a schedule break in Minneapolis, and the next day we were supposed to play an exhibition game in Sioux City (that's why I say I nearly got there after all). But now it was the night before, and I was indulging in one of my favoritest time-off habits, which is going to a good movie.

Now for some reason that I just can't explain, of all the things I've seen printed about me, this one story never came out till now. It's not a secret, or anything, but nobody up to now has pointed out that I didn't want to come to the major leagues!

I was sitting in this movie, and they knew where I was because the manager of the theater came out on the stage and said for me to get in touch with manager Tommy Heath of the Millers at the hotel.

46

I got over to the hotel, and Heath was in the room there holding his hand out and grinning.

"Congratulations!" he said.

"What for?" I said.

"You're going up to the big league."

"Who said so?"

"Leo," Heath said.

"Not me," I said. "Call up Leo and tell him I'm not coming."

Heath looked at me like I was crazy or something. Then I guess he figured I meant it, because he got on the phone and put through a long distance call to Durocher in New York.

He and Durocher talked for a couple of minutes, and then Heath said into the phone, "I don't know. I can't do anything with him. Here. I'll put him on. You talk to him."

I found myself talking to an awful mad Leo Durocher.

"What do you mean, you're not coming up?" he yelled.

"I mean it," I said. "I can't play that kind of ball."

"What do you mean by that? What can't you do?"

"Hitting," I said.

"What are you hitting for Minneapolis now?"

"Four seventy-seven."

There was a silence on the phone.

Then in sort of a subdued voice, Leo said, "Do you think maybe you can hit two-fifty for me?"

"Two-fifty?" I said. "I can try."

"Then come on up here!" he shouted.

That's how Buckduck came to the Giants.

Chapter 4

DON'T CHANGE SOCKS

I SUPPOSE there have been worse major league debuts than mine, but I don't want to hear about them.

I joined the Giants in Philadelphia on May 25, 1951. We were playing the Phillies that night at what was then Shibe Park (since that time, it's been renamed Connie Mack Stadium). Some of the Giants—Monte Irvin and Henry Thompson—I already knew, and of course, I'd met Durocher briefly in Florida.

But all of them had heard about me—thanks in the main to the New York press, which in the week previous had given me quite a build-up. I don't think all this, by any means, was caused by me. The Giants had started very slowly, and when you have a team that should be playing better than it is playing, then you're liable to hail any newcomer as the one fellow to untrack the ball club and set it going.

I met the other players only briefly that first day. Eddie Stanky, playing second base, said to me, "How do you run the bases?"

48

"I don't know," I said. "I guess I could be better."

"Watch him," he said, and pointed across the clubhouse at Monte Irvin. "He'll show you some things. Last game we played, he stole home."

"That's pretty good," I said.

"*Pretty* good?" Stanky said. "He stole home on a left-handed hitter!"

I think that was just about the first of the "little" things I've learned about baseball since I came to the majors . . . that nine times out of ten, a man who steals home does so only when there's a right-handed hitter at bat because then the batter's body blocks the catcher's view. Just think for a minute what that Irvin did—he came ninety feet to score in full view of the catcher all the way!

Monte was in right field that night against Philadelphia. Bobby Thomson, who'd been playing center, moved to left. Even today, there are red hot Giant fans who remember—as who doesn't—that season of 1951, but who insist that Durocher's big move of the year, putting Thomson on third base, happened as soon as I joined the team. Actually, the switch wasn't made until I'd been with the club nearly two months.

Well, I've stalled as long as possible. I went 5-for-0 against the Phillies. In the field, I had four routine put-outs, but on what could have been a big play, a liner that Eddie Waitkus hit to right center, I ran smack into Monte Irvin and the ball went for a double.

But we won the game 8 to 5.

In the second game of the three-game series against the Phillies, I didn't get a hit. We won the game.

That put the Giants, who'd been in fifth place when I joined them, up to .500 in the standings—won 19, lost 19. Please note that I had nothing to do with it.

The third game of the series with the Phils, I didn't get a hit. We won the game.

Now it was back to New York to face the Boston Braves. It wasn't my first time in the Polo Grounds, but it was my first as a Giant. When my name was announced as part of the batting order over the loudspeaker system, seemed like my backbone went cold all over. The fans gave me a nice hand, and that made it feel even worse. After all, here I was—up twelve times, down twelve times, and hitting tonight against a pretty fair hand named Warren Spahn.

Spahn threw me a fast ball the first time I came up against him, and I guess I must have been looking for it. I hit it on a line over the left-field roof. The ball really went. I heard later that Russ Hodges, the Giants's broadcaster who has a habit of saying "Bye-bye Baby!" when a home run goes into the stands or out of the park, took one look at that ball I hit and just plain said, "G'bye!"

So my first major-league hit was a home run. The other players whooped it up for me as I came to the dugout. We were ahead 1 to 0. But I didn't get another hit in the game, and Boston won it 4 to 1.

Matter of fact, my average after a couple more games stood at a stout .039. That home run stood as my only hit in 26 major-league at-bats.

The story is I went to Leo Durocher with tears in my eyes and begged him to send me back to the minor leagues.

I'm not sure about whether there were any tears in my eyes or not, but I sure as heck went to him.

"Get me out of there," I said.

"Why?" he said.

"I'm not hitting, that's why."

"No?" he said.

"No," I said. "Just like I told you over the phone from Minneapolis."

"Pitching any different?"

I thought about that for a minute. "No," I said finally. "There's not that much difference in the pitching."

"Okay," he said, as if that settled it.

"But I'm still not hitting," I said. "If it's not the pitching, then it must just be I'm in a slump. That still doesn't mean I'm helping you any."

"Listen," the Skipper said, "you can slump at Minneapolis as easy as you can slump up here. Have we been winning ball games since you came up?"

"Most of them," I admitted.

"Then you're my center fielder," he said, "and that's that."

I've said it a hundred thousand times, but I'll say it again, right here and now—if you can't play ball for Leo Durocher, you can't play ball for anybody.

One hit for 26 at-bats to begin with. An average of .039.

Then I got nine hits in my next 24 times up—a .375 clip!

I broke out of the slump with a single and a triple as we racked up the Pittsburgh Pirates, 14 to 3. Then, against the St. Louis Cardinals, I got two doubles and scored the only run as Dave Koslo, pitching beautifully for the Giants, won a two-hit shutout, 1 to 0.

The Giants were in third place.

Against the Cincinnati Reds, I got my second home run—a real "Chinese" drop shot down the line—off of Willard Ramsdell. In another game against the Reds I batted in three runs.

In the middle of June we were still far, far back of the league-leading Brooklyn Dodgers; but their Pee Wee Reese told one of the newspapermen, "The Giants are still the team to beat in this league." He was to prove quite some prophet.

I'd found a home in New York in Harlem, near the ball park, living with some friends from Birmingham. My off-the-field life wasn't much to write home about—of course, it shouldn't be. About the most exciting thing I did was go to movies. But the papers wanted to find some colorful copy about me, and they finally came up with some long stories about how come I always ran out from under my hat.

It's true. Running fast, either on the bases or in the field, I always seem to lose my cap, and then when the play's over, I always have to call time to go get it. When I was in Minneapolis, the papers there went the New York papers one better. They got together and offered a reward for finding a way to keep my cap on my head. Nobody's collected that reward to this day.

I got my share of ribbing through the league, too. One day against the Dodgers, Preacher Roe was pitching and I was hitting, and Roe threw a terrific strike; Roy Campanella, catching for Brooklyn, said to me, "You think he's a pretty good pitcher?"

"Sort of," I said.

"Wait till you see Newcombe tomorrow," Campy said.

Next time I came to bat, Campy started another conversation. This time I cut him short. "Durocher just told me not to talk to you," I told him.

I got needled by my teammates, too. Before the games, I was always after them to have a catch or play pepper or something, and they were always after me, too. Going to the clubhouse in center field after practice one day, Earl Rapp said to me, "Race you the rest of the way for five bucks."

"You're on," I told him, and we raced, and I beat him a good ten, fifteen feet.

"Okay," he says, panting and holding out his hand, "let's have the five."

"For what?" I said to him. "*I* beat *you*."

"Wasn't anything in the bet about anybody *beating* anybody," he said. "I just said I'd *race* you."

I threw up my hands. Sal Maglie was standing there, laughing fit to bust. "Hey, Sal," I said to him, "what do you do with a man like this?"

Maglie turned poker-face. "Pay him," he said.

Late in June we toured the western cities, and I had me a trip. I had a three-run homer in the tenth inning to win one at Chicago; at one point I had a ten-game hitting streak. All in all, on that western swing I had four home runs and sixteen runs batted in.

Back home, I tied a game in the ninth with a homer against the Phils, and then Whitey Lockman won it for us in the tenth with a long single. Whitey is, in my opinion, underrated as a hitter. He is tremendous in the clutch.

BORN TO PLAY BALL

Like Al Dark and Don Mueller and some of our other players, he has that ability to get at least a piece of the ball, and that is a great offensive advantage because it means you can have a running ball club. You can start for that next base knowing your hitter will protect you and not swing and miss and leave you hung up. There aren't too many hitters of the Lockman variety. A lot of your big hitters are so-called free swingers—they'll hit or maybe they'll miss. The 1954 Cleveland Indians were a free-swinging club in the world series against us, and that, plus the fact that we had a good throwing outfield, kept their base runners pretty close. They couldn't get that jump for the extra base.

All the way through July of '51, the Giants were still getting untracked. On July 20, Leo made his big move, transforming Bobby Thomson from an outfielder into a third baseman. That gave us two former outfielders (Thomson at third and Lockman at first) in our infield. Our second base combination was set—Dark at short and Stanky at second. Stanky was spelled occasionally by a young man named Davey Williams, who today is probably the best second baseman in the National League.

In the outfield, it was pretty regularly Irvin in left, myself in center, and Don Mueller in right. Wes Westrum handled the catching. Sal Maglie, Larry Jansen, Dave Koslo, Jim Hearn, and George Spencer were carrying the main pitching load.

At one point, as July wore into August, I had six hits in a row that were home runs—I don't mean six homers in six at-bats; I mean that out of six hits I got, six were homers. But I would have settled for strike-outs if it could have improved the team's chances any. I'd come to play winning baseball, if I could—and baseball's a game where they don't pay off on second place.

Oh, we were in second place, all right. But we were so far back of Brooklyn it wasn't even funny.

Show you how bad it was. On August 11, we were shut out by the Phillies 4 to 0, while Brooklyn was beating Boston 8 to 1 in the first game of a double header. If anybody's taken the trouble to figure the standings at that point—and later on lots of people figured it was worth the trouble—they would have read like this:

	W	L	G.B.
Brooklyn	70	35	—
New York	59	51	13½

Thirteen and a half games back with only seven weeks to go!!

Brooklyn lost the second game of that day's double header to the Braves by a score of 8 to 4.

The next day we beat the Phillies 3 to 2. It was Maglie's sixteenth victory of the season. Then Al Corwin, who was to be an important addition to the Giant pitching staff, pitched a four-hitter and the Giants beat Philadelphia again, 2 to 1.

That was a good double header to win. As one of the papers put it, "The Giants had better do some winning if they want to finish second."

On August 13, Jansen won his fifteenth, beating the Phils 5 to 2. I made a catch in that game that I still remember—a diving shoestring nab on a sinking liner from the bat of Willie Jones. Yup. My cap flew off.

Three in a row wasn't much to crow about, but we felt pretty good. All three had been pretty tight games, and we'd made some good plays—*winning* plays—instead of like some we'd made before. There had been one time, in Philadelphia at the beginning of the season, where an outfielder had caught a long foul fly with the tie-breaking run on third base and only one out. Of course, the runner loafed home to score after the catch. All the fielder had to do was let the ball drop. It was foul.

But we were playing good baseball now. We knew it, and the fans seemed to sense it. A headline in the New York *World-Telegram*, following those three straight that we took from the Phillies, said, RELAXED GIANTS MAY HAVE FUN AT LAST.

We were back in New York for a three-game series with the Dodgers. Spencer beat them in the first one 4 to 2.

And then, on August fifteenth, came a game I'll never forget. It was the game in which I made the play which *Time* Magazine called "The Throw."

We were tied with Brooklyn 1 to 1, with the Dodgers at bat and one out in the top of the eighth inning. Billy Cox, a fast man, was on third base for them, and Carl Furillo was at bat.

Furillo hit a fly ball of no more than medium depth, but he hit it to right—center field, well to my left. That meant that as a right-hander, I was traveling in the wrong direction for a throw. I would have to throw, in order to get

Cox at the plate, away from my body and away from the direction in which I was moving.

I took the ball glove-handed and made the only play that was possible. I pivoted on my left foot, swinging around so that for an instant I was facing the center-field bleachers. The full left-circle turn consumed more time, of course, than if I had been able to get the ball away while facing the plate, but it left me now in perfect throwing position.

There was a potential play at third on another runner, so Whitey Lockman was in the cut-off spot, lined up between me and the plate. I aimed on his glove and let go.

Whitey let the ball go on through. Westrum was waiting at home, caught the throw, and nailed Cox sliding in.

I don't think there's much sense in judging different plays off one against the other (for one thing, there are never two plays exactly the same) but I'll have to say I don't think I ever made a better throw. And I'm not so sure I could make the same play tomorrow. This one just happened to click.

Of all the praise I got for the throw on Cox, I think one of the nicest lines came from Chuck Dressen, the Brooklyn manager. He said, "He'll have to do it again before I'll believe it."

After the game, too, Lockman went up to Durocher and said, real straight-faced, "What would you have done if I'd cut that throw off?"

"You'd still be running," Durocher told him.

I suppose you've noticed how often a man who makes a big play in the field is first up at bat in the next inning, and how often the big play seems to be the last play of the inning. Well, maybe there are a couple of reasons for that seeming to be so. One of the reasons is that one of the things that helps make a play a big play is often that the play gets you out of the inning. The other is that if the man who made it isn't first up when his side comes to bat, the fans usually overlook it. When I was a kid in Alabama, I had a friend who lived close to the railroad tracks, and he was forever saying how this express train was always late. Fact was, it was late maybe two or three times a month, but he never paid it any mind when it was on time.

All of which proves exactly nothing at all, because that play I made on Cox ended the Dodger half of the eighth inning, and you know who was first up for the Giants in the bottom half?

Willie Mays.

No two ways about it, the fans gave me a real hand when I got up to bat. Remember, the score was still tied at 1–1.

Well, I singled. And then Mr. Westrum came up and clobbered a home run, and we won the game 3 to 1.

Two straight from Brooklyn. Then Maglie pitched a beautiful four-hitter; we won 2 to 1 to sweep the Dodger series. It was Maglie's seventeenth win of the year.

We were scheduled to come up against the Phillies for three games next. Spencer got the win as we took the first game 8 to 5. Then Jansen got off a four-hitter of his own to shut Philadelphia out 2 to 0, beating Robin Roberts in the bargain.

That was on August 19. We got to the clubhouse after

the game, and somebody said, "What'd the Dodgers do?"

We got ahold of the Brooklyn score. Brooklyn had lost to Boston.

"What was their score?" somebody asked.

"Thirteen to four," was the answer.

We looked at one another.

Al Dark said, "That means now we're eight games out of first."

Somebody else said, "That score—thirteen to four— that's some way for a pennant club to lose to the Braves!"

And somebody else said, "How many we got in a row now?"

I knew the answer to that. "Eight," I said.

"Well," they said, "if we can just sort of go along like this for maybe another week . . ."

I guess you know the old joke where one guy says to another guy, "Are you superstitious?"

And the other guy says, "Heck, no! Anybody knows that's bad luck."

Well, as a ballplayer personally, and as a ball club generally, we Giants were probably no more superstitious than the next man. Couple of little things—we'd use the same warm-up ball in practice each day, and what have you. And a couple of the guys took to wearing the same sweat shirt or the same socks.

Not that it was going to do any good. Eight in a row, and then, out to sweep the series against the Phillies, we found ourselves trailing 4 to 0 in the seventh inning.

What happened? Oh, we scored five runs and won it 5 to 4.

Then the western clubs came in to the Polo Grounds. Cincinnati was the first club in, and the Reds were ahead by a score of 4 to 2 going into the last of the eighth.

Matter of fact, it would have been 5 to 2 except that in the top of the seventh we cut down Hank Edwards trying to make it an inside-the-park home run (a real possibility at the Polo Grounds, the way the field is laid out). The thing I remember about that play is that everybody and his brother handled the ball.

Edwards had walloped one to the right-center corner. Mueller dug it out and threw to me. I threw to Whitey Lockman. Whitey relayed to Wes Westrum. Westrum cut down Edwards at the plate. Four men had handled the ball!

Way things turned out, we might as well have let Edwards have the homer.

That way, the Reds would have been leading 5 to 2 going into the last of the eighth instead of 4 to 2. For our side in the last of the eighth, Westrum, Stanky, and Lockman homered. Wes clubbed his with two men on. We won the game 7 to 4.

That was our tenth straight.

Next day we squeaked to number eleven—4 to 3 over Cincinnati.

St. Louis came in for a single-game stand, and led 5 to 4 going into the last of the ninth. The Giants scored twice and won it 6 to 5.

The baseball world was on its ear now. The fans were watching a winning streak of more than modest size, and that's always something to watch, but this was something more. In our case, they were watching a hot ball club make its move. The way Glenn Cunningham or Native Dancer would hold off the pace and then, coming into the stretch, let go.

The tennis championships had started out at Forest Hills, and we heard that the officials out there were a little upset because newspapermen covering that swank event were smuggling portable radios into the press section so they could hear how the Giants were doing. The same officials were even more upset when they found the players racing to the locker room after their matches to listen in on the Giants.

What we had coming up now were four games with the Cubs. The Cubs weren't the toughest club in the league, but they could beat you—especially when, as was the case here, those four games were to be played in the form of double-headers on two consecutive days.

We won that first double-header, 5 to 4 and 5 to 1. Fourteen in a row now.

And now we were going for fifteen—and the ball game, the first game of our second straight double-header, went into extra innings, with the score tied at 3 to 3.

Larry Jansen was pitching, going all the way, for us, but by now the strain on the ball club was tremendous. Something had to give.

It did give—it gave in the top of the twelfth, when the Cubs scored to go ahead 4 to 3.

But there was one thing we had overlooked. And that is that a club on a winning streak is not the only one to feel the stress. The team that's trying to beat you feels it too.

Like Chicago. Their defense lapsed. Not much. Just enough to help us push over two runs in the bottom of the twelfth and win it 5 to 4!

Al Corwin had it all the way in beating the Cubs 6 to 3 in the second game.

We'd won sixteen in a row. It was the longest winning streak in the National League in sixteen years, ever since back in 1935, when I was four years old!

And we'd cut eight games off the Dodger lead in the course of that streak. They hadn't been losing. They'd played .500 ball.

Obviously, our fate was in our own hands. The only trouble was, we were five games behind—and yet from here to the end of the season we would meet the Dodgers only four times, according to the schedule.

So they'd have to do some losing, too.

And even if they did, we'd have to keep on winning.

But you never saw a team so all-fired-up as ours. We'd taken sixteen in a row, and the pushover Pittsburgh Pirates were next due at the Polo Grounds. The worst, including two double-headers on consecutive days, was behind us.

So, naturally, the Pirates and Howard Pollet proceeded to shut us out, 2 to 0.

The streak was finished, but we weren't. We were the same ball club, personnel-wise. The only question we'd have to find out about was whether we could go in September, when we had a shot at the pennant, as we'd gone in August, when it looked like we didn't.

I remember one of the guys who'd worn the same pair of socks for the last week or so of the winning streak.

"Well," he said, taking them off in the clubhouse after the Pirates had beat us, "I guess I can send these to the laundry now."

"*Send* them!" Eddie Stanky said. "Criminy, just point them in the right direction and let 'em walk!"

Chapter 5

BROOKLYN BRIDGE CLOSED

IF THE Giants had lost out by a game for the National League pennant in 1951, you could have blamed one man. Me.

That first week in September, we really looked like a team. On September 1, Maglie beat the Dodgers 8 to 1 for his eighteenth victory of the season. No game had gone righter for us all year long. Don Mueller belted three—count 'em—home runs, something little short of startling, for Don doesn't specialize in the long ball. And among other things, the Giants pulled a triple play! It was one of those second-short combinations—a line drive for one out, throw to second before the runner got back for another, and just wait for that runner from first to run right into the ball for number three.

We packed 'em in at the Polo Grounds on September 2 also, and we belted the Dodgers again, 11 to 2. Mr. Mueller wrote his way into the record books by unloading two more homers!

Then we went to Philadelphia, and here's where Willie

Mays made one of the most notorious plays of his young career. I belted Roberts for an inside-the-park home run.

But I forgot to touch third base.

Actually, I'll have to take the umpire's word that I forgot to touch the base, but not even manager Durocher put up too much of a kick on the call. What seems to have happened was that, rounding third base, I just sort of glided over the sack, never touching it.

We lost the game to the Phils, 6 to 3, so of course one run for us either way didn't make the final difference. But if you look at it the way Leo did—and rightly so—after the game, it might have been all the difference in the world. We'd been getting to Roberts. A home run in that certain spot might have got him out of there, and then we'd have had a new pitcher to work on. We might have broken through.

That one defeat didn't mean the Giants were in a slump. From there we went on to beat Boston twice as Maglie took his nineteenth. Going into Ebbets Field in mid-September for our final two games with Brooklyn in the regular season, we trailed by five and a half games. We'd lost half a game from where we stood when the winning streak ended.

There'd been a curious parallel the year before, when the Phillies led the Dodgers by seven games on Labor Day and finally had to beat Brooklyn in the tenth inning of the last game of the season to save the pennant. That, though, was a case of a first-place team falling apart. The Phils, a young club that no one gave a chance for the pennant, had been held up mainly in 1950 by the pitching of Roberts, Curt Simmons, and Jim Konstanty. In that September stretch drive, Simmons's National Guard unit was called up. Without him, the Phils couldn't take up the slack. Luckily, time and key last-game pitching by Roberts and hitting by Dick Sisler were on their side. If the season had gone another week, they would have been out of it. That's a likely guess anyway—and a good guess, considering the way they lost the world series to the Yankees in four straight.

Now, in 1951, the situation, standings-wise and time-wise, was just about the same. But here, the club in first place wasn't slumping. It was just that the club coming on was hot.

The thing about it was that now we had only two games left with the Dodgers. We had to take both games. Everybody knew that.

There was a standing-room-only crowd at Ebbets Field for the first game, and Brooklyn defeated the Giants 9 to 0 behind two-hit pitching by Don Newcombe!

Six and a half games behind now. But the papers and, generally, the fans too, knew it wasn't a race any more. The Giants had put up a gallant run, but it was a good old case of too little and too late.

So the crowd wasn't capacity for the second game—our last against Brooklyn.

Maglie won it for us, 2 to 1, for his twentieth win of the year.

The big blow of the game was a Monte Irvin home run, but the big play was a sensational fielding stunt by Bobby Thomson, who'd been a third baseman less than two months.

We were ahead 2 to 1 in the last of the eighth, but with

one out, Brooklyn had Jackie Robinson on third base and Andy Pafko at bat. The combination was enough to scare you out of your spikes. Not only was Pafko an always-dangerous hitter, but Robinson was, without doubt, the most dangerous man in all of baseball when it came to leading off third base. He could dance a pitcher nuts.

Maglie paid him no mind, though. That Maglie is at his best in a jackpot game against the Dodgers—and make no mistake about it, this was a jackpot game. Everybody except the players, it seemed, had just about quit on the Giants after Newcombe beat them. If we'd lost this one too, we might have started to think that way also.

Anyway, Maglie pitched the ball and Pafko slashed one down the third-base line on one wicked hop. Thomson was there—somehow—to stab the ball. He reached out, and all in one motion tagged Robinson off of third and fired to first for the double play on Pafko. It was a sensational play.

All right. We were still in it. We won, and then we won some more. "All right," Leo Durocher said in the clubhouse one day, with still more than a week to go in the pennant race, "what do I do now?"

Ed Stanky said, "What's the problem?"

"I can't eat, that's the problem," the Skip said. "I can't keep any food on my stomach." And he barged on into his private office.

At one point, we'd won twenty-nine out of thirty-five games. Jansen beat the Braves 4 to 1 for his twenty-first win of the year. We beat the Braves again, 4 to 3 this time, and now we trailed the Dodgers by two and a half games.

The thirty-fourth Giant victory in forty-one games was a 5 to 1 win over the Phillies on September 25.

Then the news came in from Boston.

The Dodgers had lost a double-header!!

There were three days left in the season. We had to win another. We did. The Dodgers had to lose another. They did.

And going into the final Saturday we were tied for the lead.

New York City had been biting its fingernails up to now—the Yankees had already clinched their pennant in the American League, so it would be an all–New York world series no matter what—but at this point the big town blew its top.

Baseball writer Howard Sigmand said it all in a round-up story, starting it off with: "They closed the Brooklyn Bridge today—at both ends."

That final week of the season was just unbelievable. Even the New York *Times* started slapping the ball scores on page one. At the Pep-Saddler title fight at the Polo Grounds, on a night we were winning at Philadelphia, they announced the inning scores between rounds, and it got a bigger yell than the fight did.

On that final Saturday, we beat the Braves 3 to 0. Maglie won his twenty-third. On one base-running sequence, I stole second, then third.

The Dodgers won too, but now we weren't worried. We could *win* this pennant. All we had to do was beat Boston on Sunday and hope Brooklyn lost to Philadelphia. If Brooklyn won its game, then we had a head-on crack at them in a best-out-of-three play-off series.

Well, we won that game in Boston, won it 3 to 2 for Jansen's twenty-second. And that was the game where I got the greatest fielding thrill of my career.

Brooklyn was losing—losing bad—to Philadelphia. Boston had its last chance in the ninth inning, and with two out, the hitter—I think it was Sid Gordon—lifted an easy fly ball toward Monte Irvin in straightaway left field.

I went racing over from center as fast as my legs would go. I still don't know what I thought I was going to do about anything. Monte was there, waiting. I shouted at him. He patted his glove a couple of times. I shouted some more. Then Monte made the catch. I jumped on him out of just plain joy.

By the time we got to the train going back to New York, Brooklyn was losing to Philadelphia by five or six runs, and it was along about the eighth inning.

We got periodic bulletins on the train. Some way, somehow, Brooklyn had tied the score. Then the game went into extra innings. The Phils loaded the bases with none out. Brooklyn got out of it. Jackie Robinson made one of the most fantastic plays of his career, going sprawling to snatch a line drive out of the air. Then, in the top of the fourteenth inning, that same Robinson hit a home run, and Brooklyn won the game.

That meant we'd have to have a play-off.

And the Giants were no worse than even money.

It had been uphill all the way, beginning with an eleven-game losing streak at the very start of the season, but now we were going like a runaway freight. We'd won 37 of our last 44 games. Know what percentage that kind of ball is? Eight-forty, that's what. Sure, our 16-game winning streak was part of it, but don't forget we'd also won 12 of our final 13 games—and our last 7 in a row.

In fact, from the start of that 44-game stretch back on August 12, the Brooklyn Dodgers had played *winning baseball!* They'd played 48 games from August 12 on, won 26 of them, lost 22, for a .540 pace. In other words, they didn't exactly fold. We had to go out and catch them. Even the miracle Braves of 1914, who came from last place to win the pennant, didn't do what the 1951 Giants did, because those Braves began to climb on July 4. We didn't make our move till more than a month later, when time was beginning to run out.

We had something else going for us, too. As soon as a play-off seemed possible, the National League had officials from the two teams flip a coin to decide the play-off sites. The Giants won the toss. The scheme of the play-off in the National League was that one team would be host for the first game, then the other would get the second game and, if necessary, the third game, too. So president Horace Stoneham of the Giants elected to let the Dodgers have the opener at Ebbets Field. That meant we'd have two out of three shots at them in our own ball park if it went that far.

It was only the third play-off in major league history, and the second in our league. All three play-offs were post–World War II. In 1946, those same Dodgers lost to the Cardinals. And over in the American League, where the play-off is limited to just one game, the Indians defeated the Red Sox the day after the season ended in 1948.

It was Jim Hearn for us, Ralph Branca for them in the

play-off opener at Ebbets Field. The game was quick and to the point. We won the game 3 to 1. Hearn pitched a five-hitter. Monte Irvin, who'd hit 23 homers on the season (I had 20), and who led the league in runs batted in with 121, homered off of Branca. Earlier Bobby Thomson, who had hit 30 home runs in the regular season and batted in 101 runs, cuffed Branca for a two-run homer.

Any baseball fan can tell you that Thomson homered off of Branca in that '51 play-off, but few of them remember that he did it in the first game—too.

Boy, we were a happy bunch of Giants after that win in the play-off opener. We only needed one more victory, had two games to get it in, and both games would be at our park. Furthermore, that Dodger-killing Maglie was ready, although there was a world series coming up, too. For the second game of the play-off, Leo Durocher decided not to use "the Barber," as Maglie, whose beard grows fast and dark, is known. If we won, Maglie could start the world series for us. If we lost, he could pitch the rubber game of the play-off. Either way, he'd get an extra day's rest. He'd pitched Saturday. This was Tuesday.

But in that clubhouse after that Monday victory we were really happy. Our latest winning streak was eight in a row now—38 out of 45, 13 of our last 14. I came in for a real stretch of horseplay. One of the players—I think it was Lockman—came over and said, "That girl's on the phone."

I said, "What girl?"

"Cut it out," he said, and made with the eyes.

"I don't know what you're talking about," I said.

71

"Listen," he said, "I don't mean to pry in your affairs. You can keep it a secret if you want. But she's on the phone. Better go talk to her."

I went over to the phone, and Durocher was there.

"What're you doing?" he said to me.

"Phone call for me," I said.

"Who is it?"

"I don't know."

"Is it a girl?"

"Yes," I said.

"But you don't know who it is?"

"No."

"You've got so many of them, is that it?"

"All I know is, it's a girl on the phone."

The Skip reached over and hung up the phone. "You know the club rule on that."

"What rule?" I said.

"I ought to fine you a hundred," Durocher said. "This one time I'll let you off. Go take your shower."

I went into the shower room, and the next thing you know another one of the players came in and tapped me on the shoulder.

"Phone for you," he said. "It's a girl."

"Man," I said to him, "why can't you leave me be? I'm just a boy, only twenty years old."

"That's right," he said solemnly. "I forgot. I thought you played center field for the Giants."

Don't think I'm wandering from the subject at hand when I say that two days after we clinched the 1954 pennant, we played the Brooklyn Dodgers, with nothing

72

at stake, and lost to a rookie left-hander named Karl Spooner. He struck out fifteen of us Giants.

After the game, Westrum said to me, "Who'd he remind you of?"

"Labine," I said.

We were both thinking of that second play-off game of '51 against the Dodgers. The Dodger pitcher was Clem Labine. Like Spooner three years later, Labine was new to us. We didn't know what he could throw.

And by the time we found out, that ball game was done and over a year and more. The Dodgers pasted the hay out of us. They whipped us 10 to 0, squaring the play-off at a victory apiece.

Strangely, we didn't feel too badly about it. It's different when you get beat one run or on a close play. And it works the other way around, too. I once heard Johnny Mize, the former Cardinal, Giant, and Yankee first baseman, put a lot of wisdom into an offhand remark. Somebody, talking about some club that was driving for the pennant, said, "What that team needs is a real big win—15 to 2, or something like that—to take the pressure off. They've had to squeak through game after game."

And Mize said, "I'd say that's the way to win them—squeaking through. If you win it big, maybe you get the idea you can do it again, and then you let up just a little. By the time you pull out of it, maybe you've lost yourself a ball game you didn't have to lose."

Anyway, the reporters all gathered around Leo Durocher in our clubhouse following that pasting we took from the Dodgers and Labine.

The Skipper was right to the point. "No chances we

73

blew," he said, "no one play that broke the game open, no nothing. We just got the pants kicked off of us."

So it all came down to that final Wednesday, with Maglie going for us, Don Newcombe going for them.

The Dodgers grabbed a run in the first. Some faulty base-running cost us a shot at scoring in an early inning, and it wasn't till the seventh inning that we scored off of Newcombe to get even.

Score tied 1–1 now, but it didn't stay that way long. Helped by a couple of line hits down the third-base line and into that tricky left-field corner at the Polo Grounds, the Dodgers scored three times in the top of the eighth.

We didn't score in our half of the eighth. With Larry Jansen in to spell Maglie, they didn't score in the top of the ninth.

The twin scoreboards in right and left fields both told the same story:

Brooklyn	1	0	0	0	0	0	0	3	0
New York	0	0	0	0	0	0	1	0	

Monte Irvin and I were the last ones in to the dugout from the field as the teams changed sides, left and center fields being the farthest away from the Giant dugout at the Polo Grounds. Usually by the time I got in to the bench from center field, Durocher already was on his way out to the third-base coaching box.

This time, though, he was standing on the dugout steps, waiting till everybody got in.

Then he turned around and faced us, leaning in on us with one hand up on the roof of the dugout, and looking

74

from one face to the next. I never saw a calmer-looking guy.

"Well," he said, sort of reflectively, "you've come this far. It's an awful long way to come. And you've still got a chance to hit." And then he went on out to the coaching box, with that number 2 still looking big and jaunty on his back.

Alvin Dark led off for us and slapped a hard grounder to the right side. Second baseman Jackie Robinson and first baseman Gil Hodges scissored across, Robinson the deep man, and for an instant we couldn't tell what would happen. But the ball was through between them and into right field for a single.

Now Don Mueller stepped in. He hit an almost identical shot—a little more to the right, maybe, but Hodges was playing him over that way, so the difference was the same. Again Robinson gave it the deep try and again the ball was through. Dark stopped at second, taking no chances with the score 4 to 1 against us in the last of the ninth.

Irvin, our big hitter, came to bat now. Out in the Dodger bull pen, three pitchers were working like crazy. A home run now—well, it was crazy even to think about it, but it would tie the score.

But Monte put up a meek foul fly to the right side, and there was one out. You should have seen the way Irvin slammed that bat down. He was sick over it.

That brought Lockman to bat. And for the third time in the game he sliced a double to left field. This one zipped past Cox at third. Dark tore around to score from second. Mueller, facing a potential play at third, slid so hard into

75

third base that he sprained his ankle—so severe a sprain that he had to be carried from the field on a stretcher.

Red Smith wrote in his column the next day that the scene at that point—stretcher bearers—seemed the perfect final touch.

Clint Hartung went in to run for Mueller, so he was leading off third, Lockman off second, as Bobby Thomson stepped to the plate. We were behind 4 to 2 now, with one out and the tying runs both in scoring position.

Time was held up now as the Dodgers changed pitchers. Manager Dressen consulted with his bull pen coach by phone and then gave Branca the wave. Newcombe shook Branca's hand solemnly and then was cheered as he made the long walk to the clubhouse in center field.

This change of pitchers, by the way, was the only managerial move in the inning, before or after. Obviously, Irvin wasn't bunting when he came to bat, even though the situation was two on and none out, because we didn't need those two runs. We needed three even to tie. And now there were men on second and third with one down, a situation that frequently calls for the intentional base on balls, but the Dodgers's lead was down to two runs now, at 4 to 2, and they weren't going to put that winning run on base.

I don't know if they were looking past Thomson or not. If they had been, then they knew that the next man in the batting order was Willie Mays.

As it was, I was down on one knee there in the on-deck circle as Branca finished his warm-up throws and Thomson stepped in to face him.

Bobby didn't offer at the first pitch, which cut the

76

center of the plate. Umpire Lou Jorda, back of the plate, sang out, "Strike one!"

From where I was, the next pitch didn't look quite so good as the first one, but Thomson swung anyway. He socked it out toward left field, and I remember thinking, *This'll get the run in from third.* I watched left fielder Pafko as he went back to the wall and turned.

And Pafko just stood there, back to the wall.

I think maybe I was the last man in that whole ball park to realize the ball was a home run.

The next thing I knew, seemed like the whole Giant team had rushed past me so they could all group around home plate, waiting for Bobby to get there. I still hadn't moved.

I started saying to myself, *It's the pennant! It's the pennant!* Maybe I still didn't believe it.

But then I got a look at the Dodgers walking off the field.

And brother, then I believed it.

I still don't know how Thomson managed to get off that field alive. The fans just plain came cascading out of the stands. It was the wildest mob scene you ever laid eyes on. Even after we got to the clubhouse, the fans, a great big crowd of them, stayed on the field outside the clubhouse windows and kept on hollering and cheering, and finally Bobby went out to the top of the clubhouse steps to wave to them. They'd be there yet if he hadn't.

The biggest thrill I ever got from a home run? That was it right there. I never got a bigger kick from a homer in my life than from that one I watched from the on-deck circle.

And, like I said before, my biggest fielding thrill was that routine fly ball that Irvin caught in that final game of the regular season up in Boston. In the clubhouse after we finally took the pennant, a newspaperman came up to me and said, "I've been meaning to ask you. What was it you were yelling at Irvin while he was waiting for that fly ball to come down in that Boston game? You were running towards him and hollering your head off."

"Gee," I told him, "I don't know. Why don't you ask Irvin?"

The reporter called Monte over and asked him. Monte started to laugh.

"He yelled out, 'Catch it!'" Monte said. "'Catch it or I'll kill you!'"

I said, "You caught it, didn't you?"

"Doggone right," Monte said.

Chapter 6

PVT. MAYS, CENTER FIELD

LOOKING back, it's a funny thing. It seems like that time I spent in the on-deck circle waiting for Bobby Thomson to hit that home run lasted a lot longer than the next two and a half years did.

Looking back now, those two and a half years went awful fast. It seems like one minute Thomson was hitting that home run to win the 1951 pennant and the next minute we were ready to start the 1954 season.

In between, of course, a lot happened. It started with the '51 world series. Between the series money and my base salary with the Giants that year, which was $7,500, I found out it was possible to make more than $10,000 in one year . . . and from doing what you liked to do. I hadn't given it much thought before that, but there it was.

That first world series of mine was a terrific thrill, even though I had no business even being in the same ball park with somebody like Joe DiMaggio.

Over the whole series, I got four hits, all singles, in twenty-two at-bats, for a miserable .182 average. The

79

Giants as a team did quite a bit better than that. That was a good Yankee team that year—a *great* Yankee team— and naturally they were favored to win. But we took them six games, and we were leading two games to one with a good chance to make it three to one when the fourth game was postponed because of rain. At that point, Casey Stengel's pitching rotation was down to where he had to rely on Johnny Sain in that fourth game. The Yankees had picked Sain up from the Braves late in the season, so we Giants would have had a chance to hit pitching that we were familiar with. But rain gave Stengel the extra day he needed, and we never did see Sain except for a two-inning relief bit. And that was a real switch on the famous formula that won the pennant for the Braves back in 1948—"Spahn and Sain and a day of rain."

The fans felt sorry for us generally because they figured, as did the newspapers, that the tension of that high-pressure race and play-off would leave us too tired to give the Yankees much of a fight. Actually, if anything, we were lifted up, not tired. The play-off had extended three days past the end of the season, so there was no waiting time between our victory and the start of the world series. Barely twenty hours after Thomson hit the homer, Allie Reynolds was throwing the first pitch of the series. We couldn't have worried about the Yankees even if we'd wanted to. We just didn't have the time. Furthermore, we were still so high up in the clouds from Thomson's clout that we just plain were feeling no pain.

The thing that did hurt us was the loss of Mueller, whose sprained ankle kept him out of the series. But that was a physical loss. I don't buy that theory that says the well-rested team wins the series. Look at the postwar years for proof:

In 1945, the Tigers didn't clinch till the final day of the year, but beat the Cubs, who'd clinched earlier, in the series. In 1946, the Red Sox ran away with the American League, winning by about fifteen games, while the Cardinals went into a post-season play-off with the Dodgers. The Cards won the series. In 1947, the Yanks and Dodgers clinched about the same times and the series went seven games. In 1948, the Braves clinched fairly early but the Indians had to win a post-season play-off from the Red Sox to nail their pennant. The Indians took the series. In 1949, both the Yankees and Dodgers clinched on the last day of the season, but the Yanks had to come from behind under pressure whereas the Dodgers were running out the string from on top, and the Yanks went on to win the series with ease. You'd have to come up to 1950 to find a year that went the other way, with the Phils going to the last day of the season before clinching, and then losing the series in four straight to the Yanks. But here the loss of Simmons was the key factor.

Matter of fact, I not only don't buy the theory that the well-rested club has the advantage—I think it runs a real chance of being at a disadvantage. Once you've let down, sometimes it's hard to get back up. Often in the world series it's not so much a case of one club playing better than it should as it is of the other club, frequently a well-rested club, playing not so good as it can.

And you should have seen the way the '51 Giants went in that world series opener against the Yanks at Yankee Stadium. I'd never before played before a crowd that big—it was 70,000. But, as I say, we were feeling no pain at all. With two out in the first inning, Henry Thompson walked, went to second as Monte Irvin singled to left, and scored as Whitey Lockman doubled to left. And while the Yankees were taking a good look at the redoubtable Mr. Bobby Thomson, waving his bat at Reynolds as he waited for the pitch—why, Monte Irvin stole home!

Monte got four hits and had another taken away from him in that opening game. Dave Koslo pitched all the way for us, and in the sixth inning Al Dark belted a three-run homer. We won it 5 to 1.

Three infield hits and a drop-shot home run by Joe Collins won for the Yankees in the second game, back of Ed Lopat, 3 to 1. Mickey Mantle twisted his knee running for a fly ball and that was the last we saw of the Yankees' star rookie in the series.

I had two hits and one run batted in—my only one of the series—as we won a wild third game back of Jim Hearn, 6 to 2. That was the game of the celebrated "drop-kick," in which the Yankees claimed that our Eddie Stanky, sliding into what seemed a sure put-out at second base, kicked the ball out of Phil Rizzuto's hand and, as the ball rolled into the outfield, got up and continued to third. Rizzuto had a funny line about that when he appeared on a TV show a few nights later.

"What about that drop-kick play?" the announcer asked him. "Did Stanky kick the ball out of your hand or not?"

"Who cares about that?" Rizzuto replied. "All I know is he hasn't touched second base yet!"

82

There followed that rainy Sunday, and on Monday DiMaggio smacked a two-run homer in the fifth inning as we lost 6 to 2. By Tuesday, Lopat was ready again for them. He's quite a pitcher, wonderful on control and little changes in speed. Yogi Berra, the Yankee catcher, told Casey Stengel after the game—which the Yanks won 13 to 1 with the then-rookie Gil McDougald becoming the first freshman ever to hit a grand-slam homer in the series—anyway, Berra told manager Stengel that he didn't have to call a single pitch from Lopat after the fourth inning. Stengel grinned at him. "Yogi," he said, "it was the best game you caught all year."

We were down three games to two in the series now. We lost the sixth game of the series 4 to 3. Hank Bauer made a good on-his-knees catch of a liner by pinch hitter Sal Yvars to end our last threat in the ninth inning. Bauer had also tripled for three runs to clinch it for the Yanks.

I'll never forget the late inning in which Stengel sent a pinch runner in for DiMaggio who was on third base. I think the fans must have realized the truth—that this was DiMag's last game of baseball. They stood and gave him a tremendous ovation as he walked to the dugout.

Going home to Birmingham was quite an experience. I wanted to see the family, and also I had a date with my draft board on October 20, after which I planned to do some barnstorming. But it seemed like everybody I met wanted to know what it was like when Thomson hit the home run. And everytime I started to tell them, they'd interrupt me to tell me what *they* were doing when Thomson got the homer.

83

BORN TO PLAY BALL

For a time, it looked like I wouldn't be going in the Army. There was a question of an aptitude test, which I had to re-take, and then the question of dependents. By now I was contributing regularly to the support of my father, my Aunt Sarah, and my half brothers and sisters. When it was all over, though, I was scheduled for induction anyway. I was glad I'd be going in at the age of twenty-one (actually, I was drafted two days short of my twenty-first birthday). That meant I'd be drafted young, instead of, say, in the middle of a baseball career. Other fellows didn't have it so lucky.

I didn't go into the Army until May 29, 1952, which meant I had both spring training and the first thirty-four games of the regular season under my belt. I'd just as soon forget that spring training. We were playing the Indians in an exhibition game at Denver when Monte Irvin, going from first to third when I singled behind him, broke his ankle sliding into third base.

I was so upset that it made me sick. Monte and I were more than good friends—we were roommates whenever the team was on the road. Still are. Like Frank Forbes, the New York athletic official who sort of took me under his wing and showed me the ropes, and Mrs. David Goosby, who was sort of my housemother in 1954—I had a room in her five-room apartment in Harlem, and she'd look out to see I was getting enough sleep and not reading too many comic books. Like them, that's how Monte was. He's married, and kind of a steady, quiet guy. All through the 1954 season we played Boss of the Room when we were on the road. The guy who got the most base hits that day was Boss of the Room till the next day. He had

84

to buy all the soda for the other guy, only the other guy had to drink it all up. No putting it off till the next day.

Monte would always make out like he hated me because I wouldn't let him sleep in the morning, but that's just because he's unusual. Me, I like to sleep as much as anybody. Eight hours a night. And after a night game, that means I wouldn't necessarily be getting up very early in the morning. Only thing was, I'd get up ahead of *Irvin*.

First year I was up with the Giants, when I was living in a seven-room railroad flat with some friends I'd known from back in Alabama, I got me a Pontiac, because that's what Irvin drove. Then in 1954 I got me a Lincoln Capri. I bought my dad a car with part of my world series money. I like to drive. I kept a car in the Army, but of course there wasn't as much use for it there, so it sort of became the company car and anybody drove it who was off.

On the road, too, Irvin always pretended he was sore about me always matching him to see who paid for dinner, because he said I eat more than he does. I'm pretty strictly meat-and-potato, but I do like to eat. Especially in the season, you're generally limited to two big meals a day—bacon and eggs and potatoes and milk for breakfast, and then either afternoon before a night game or suppertime after a day game, another big meal. A steak or a nice chicken or some chops. And Irvin was always yelling at me about I liked to go to too many movies, or I was playing too many King Cole records on the portable phonograph I take around on trips, or I packed too many clothes because I didn't want to wear anything that had a spot on it or was mussed up or like that.

First thing Monte said to me when I joined the Giants,

85

coming up from Minneapolis in 1951, was, "You play golf?"

That's because I'd walked in the clubhouse with a golf bag that the Minneapolis fans had given me for a going-away present. I had to unzip the golf bag and show him that I was using it to carry my bats in. I stick to one kind of bat, by the way. It's an Adirondack model, made by McLaughlin Millard, 35 inches in length, 34 ounces in weight. I hold it pretty much down at the end of the bat.

"Well," Irvin said, "Where do you keep your golf clubs?"

"I don't play golf," I said.

"What do you play, besides baseball?"

"Knock rummy," I said, "and pool. And pinball."

Monte started to laugh. "You any good at pinball?"

"They call me No-Tilt Willie," I told him.

Irvin always had a word of advice or two about girls, too, whenever I had any problems. In '51 and '54 I dated a good bit, but never going steady with any one girl. One time Frank Forbes got wind of an older woman who decided she was going to latch on for me and went into an ice-cream parlor where she knew I came in a lot and waited for me there. Forbes came in the place just after I got there and knocked the woman's ice cream into her lap.

"I was just doing it for your sake," he said later. "You're not sore, are you?"

"No," I said, "but I can't get over it. I never saw such a mess in all my born days."

If Irvin didn't have a house in New Jersey, where he

lives when the team's playing at home, I'd have him playing stickball on St. Nicholas Place in Harlem. Stickball is strictly a New York game. You use a tough little rubber ball, like a handball, and the pitcher throws it on the bounce and what you usually hit it with is a broomstick. You run bases like in baseball. You usually use a hydrant or the fender of a parked car for the bases. Distance is measured in manhole covers (or, as we call them, sewers). Nights during the summer, when it stays light till after eight o'clock, I can almost always pick up a game with some of the kids on the block. It's not only fun, it's good for the batting eye, swinging with that thin stick at that tiny ball.

Anyway, I got talking about this because I was talking about Monte Irvin, and I got talking about Monte because of when he broke his leg. He was out most of that season.

Personally, I only got into 34 games before it was time to leave for the Army, and I was only hitting .236. But the Giants had won 27 of their first 34 games. They were in first place at the time. I'm not the one to judge what my going away meant to them, but you have to figure that no ball club can lose two out of three of its regular outfielders and have the same over-all strength. By the time Irvin could play again, it was too late for a run at the pennant, and the Giants finished second.

I did my Army hitch at Camp Eustis, Virginia, where we had a ball club and I got to play in about 180 games. We had some good men—Verne Law, a pitcher with Pittsburgh, and Karl Olson, a Red Sox outfielder, were among them. And playing against another Army team,

I got to look at a pretty fair pitcher—young fellow named Johnny Antonelli. On our team, too, was Jimmy Ludtka, a second baseman from the Piedmont League, who became a good buddy of mine.

I played basketball at Camp Eustis, too, and I don't think Leo Durocher liked that idea too much. He figured I could get hurt. Matter of fact, I did sprain my ankle in baseball; and another time I stole a base with our team out in front 14 to 0. I hear Leo like to go wild.

I was assigned to the physical training department at Camp Eustis and did a lot of instruction work.

While I was at it, there was something I taught myself.

As I'll tell in the next chapter, where we'll study what it's like to play center field in the big leagues, one of the big things with me is getting the ball back to the infield as fast as possible once I make a catch. Most outfielders make their throws from the back-of-the-ear throwing position. Most of my throws, though, are made from lower down and farther out from the body, tending toward the sidearm. It occurred to me I could save a fraction of time by catching the ball lower down, too.

That was when I started to work on my "basket" or "vest-pocket" catch—where, instead of having the hands up in front of the face, thumbs in, I held them at midriff height, thumbs out.

At the same time, I worked to perfect a first-baseman-type hold on my glove. That divides the glove into two parts—the thumb part and the rest of the mitt. The thumb and the rest of the fingers hold their parts in a sort of pincer grip, at the very heel of the glove. The rest of the hand isn't in the glove at all. That means the hand is used only to control the glove. The pocket where the ball hits doesn't have any of me in it at all.

The purpose of this isn't to keep my hand from hurting when a hard liner smacks in there. The purpose is, instead, to add two or three inches of reach onto my gloved hand.

That's the way I do it. I don't definitely recommend either that kind of grip or the "basket" kind of catch as a general thing for outfielders. You may find that you field grounders much more easily by having your hand in the glove the regular way. And the way you throw will make the difference as to the way you should make a catch.

As time went on in the Army, the Giants were having their troubles. Second place in 1952, they fell to fifth in '53, losing 44 of their final 64 games and ending up 35 games off the pennant. I was itching to get back. When the following March came and I was mustered out, Frank Forbes was there waiting for me at the gate to drive to Washington and from there to fly to our spring training quarters in Arizona.

It was an unexpectedly cold day, and Forbes lent me his overcoat and then stuffed a couple of newspapers up inside his shirt to keep himself warm. We made quite a sight driving up to the Washington airport, especially since that was the day some revolutionists had shot up the House of Representatives.

At Phoenix there were many changes waiting for me. That guy Antonelli was pitching for us now! Gone was Bobby Thomson, traded to Milwaukee, but pitcher Don Liddle was there, and another pitcher named Windy McCall. Marv Grissom was new to me, and I was introduced to a real good guy named Dusty Rhodes who, I was told, went absolutely crazy with a bat every now and again so you couldn't get him out.

Leo Durocher didn't even say hello to me. He just stared at me dead pan and said, "Intra-camp game today. You ready?"

"No curve balls," I said.

"Nothing *but* curve balls," he said.

Then Bobby Hofman came over and said, "Hi, there. You been away?"

"Cut it out," I said.

"New pitching in the league," Sal Maglie said. "You better find somebody to fill you in."

"*You* fill me in," I said.

"I'm too busy getting in shape," Sal said.

"Boy," I said, "what a bunch of guys you are."

Somebody came up and snapped a towel at me. I heard Durocher telling a newspaperman, "If he hits two eighty and gets twenty home runs, that's all I'm going to ask."

"Hey!" I yelled over at him. "I'm not going to hit any two eighty."

"That reminds me," he yelled back, "you owe me sixty dozen Cokes from two years ago!"

"What for?" I yelled.

"You know what for!" he yelled back.

I didn't have the slightest idea what for.

But I tell you, there wasn't a place on the face of the earth I'd have rather been than that Giant clubhouse. I went outside and belted one over the fence first time up. It was like coming home again.

Chapter 7

MR. YOU, CENTER FIELD

Time out for a minute from talking about me. Let's talk about you instead.

You want to play outfield, you say.

All right. Let's go out there and field a few.

We'll leave hitting out of this for the time being, and concentrate on defense.

Maybe it'll surprise you to learn that, of the five most important things that go into making a good defensive outfielder, you already have *all five!*

I'm not talking about running, or fielding, or throwing. Some people do these better than others, but they are things that can be improved by practice. The more you practice, the more you'll improve. There's no two ways about that.

But those five important things I was talking about— you can do those right now.

Here's the list:

1. Be alert.
2. Keep your eye on the ball.

3. Anticipate your play.
4. Know your hitter.
5. GET RID OF THE BALL!

An outfielder who can do all five of these has got to be classed as a good defensive outfielder regardless of how fast he can run or how far he can throw!

Let's say you're a pitcher. Wouldn't you be pretty pleased to know you had a man in center field whom you could trust to backstop on any pick-off throw, catch a fly ball with certainty, throw to the right base, play in the right position, and get the ball back fast? You sure would! And you wouldn't trade him for another player who maybe could run a little faster or throw a little harder, but who was lacking in one or more of those essentials.

But let's go a little further. Let's break those categories down and see what makes them tick. Here we go.

1. *Be alert.* The thing to realize first off here is a great defensive outfield is usually measured over a season not so much by the things it does as by the things it doesn't have to do. The New York Giants of 1954 had an outfield that was alert, fast, and good-throwing. In the first game of the world series the Cleveland Indians left thirteen runners on base. In the second game they left thirteen more. Throughout the series they had a total of more runners on base than we did—even though we beat them four straight.

All right. It's evident that those runners couldn't have done much advancing on the bases. And yet there wasn't a single play in the whole series where an Indian was cut down coming into home plate or third base.

By and large, that spells it out—they weren't *trying* to

92

advance! They weren't taking any chances on the bases—not from any lack of desire to win, certainly, but because they must have figured it was too risky.

Now there are two ways to keep a man from going to third from first on a single. One is to throw him out at third. The other is to see him stop at second. One way's just as good as the other. But that's what I mean when I say that a good outfield can be measured by the things it doesn't have to do.

The chief element here is being alert. In the fourth inning of the first game of that same world series, Cleveland had a man on second with two out and we tried a pick-off where the throw was a little bit off. The ball trickled into center field.

I was in there to backstop the play. The runner, who under other conditions could have gone to third, stayed where he was.

There's a classic story that fits in here about Hack Wilson, the old National League home-run champion, who dozed off one day while playing out in that shallow right field in the old Baker Bowl in Philadelphia. Standing there with his hands resting on his knees, Wilson sort of closed his eyes for a little catnap.

Just about then, his manager decided to change pitchers. The decision angered the outgoing pitcher, and on a sudden impulse he took the ball and threw it at the close-in right field wall.

The sound of the ball hitting the wall brought Wilson instantly to life again. Turning, he fielded the ball and threw it on a line to second base.

On the positive side, I'd say that an outfielder who's

alert can save up to four or five games a season on alert play alone. On the negative side, an outfielder who's not alert can cost his club the same number of games. There's a ten-game difference right there. But aside from that, the mere fact that the other team knows you're on the hustle out there all the time is a very definite part of what goes into helping your team. There's no telling how much good it will do. But don't kid yourself. More bases are run in terms of what the runner *thinks* the defense can do than most people realize.

Being alert means a lot more than just backing up on pick-off plays. An alert outfielder will notice how wide a turn an enemy hitter makes at first base after a single . . . maybe there's a shot there for a throw back to first. He'll notice what kind of pitches are being thrown. He'll know when the pitch-out is called. He'll react automatically to help form the defensive pattern for a relay throw on a deep hit to another field; he'll back up other outfielders. When a rundown play unfolds in the infield, especially when, with more than one man on base, some of the infielders have to deploy to protect against a further advance if the rundown fails, your alert outfielder is already headed for the infield on the dead run to help out. You rarely see an outfielder actually participate in a rundown (for one thing, rundowns usually work), but it's not at all uncommon to see an outfielder station himself at an otherwise unguarded base during the course of a rundown—just in case. Here's a quick example: Say there are men on second and third and the pitcher, catcher, and third baseman become involved in running down the man off third. The pattern then is for the first baseman to cover home, the second baseman to cover second, the shortstop to cover third. Offhand, it would seem that first base could be left unmanned, since there was no runner there to begin with, but that reckons without the man who hit the ball that started the rundown. An alert right fielder will cover first base in a case of this kind.

Even more of an occasion for an outfielder to cover an infield base comes along when a couple of infielders leave their position to chase a ball in foul territory. This can be an important covering pattern, especially in parks like Forbes Field in Pittsburgh, or the Polo Grounds and Yankee Stadium in New York, where there is a lot of room between the foul lines and the stands in the infield and home-plate area.

2. *Keep your eye on the ball.* Late in 1954, a columnist in a New York paper said that more sandlotters than ever were dropping fly balls that season—because they all were imitating Willie Mays's "basket" catch. Well, they say imitation is the sincerest form of flattery. I don't know where that writer got his statistics on how many fly balls were being dropped in sandlot games, but assuming he's correct about it, I still can't take either the credit or the blame.

As I said earlier, I have a special reason for using the catch I use, and I don't recommend it by any means as the only way to catch a fly ball. But if more players drop the ball using my catch instead of the hands-up, thumbs-in, standard kind, the only reason is that they had a little longer in which to take their eye off the ball.

Never take your eye off the ball!

"Oh, no?" you say. "What about you? What about the

catch you made on Wertz in the world series with your back to the plate?"

If you're going to ask that question, then I'd better tell you that I looked up at the last minute to locate the ball. I'd have never made the catch if I didn't. I've never seen those plays you hear about where an outfielder chased a ball a country mile and then stuck up his glove, still not looking, and there it was.

It is not only permissible, it's *necessary* at times to look away from the ball *after you have gauged its flight*. This is something that has to be done in two situations: (1) where the ball has to be run for over a sizable distance, and (2) where you have to contend with a wall or some other barrier. In the first case, you can't attain top running speed with your head up at some whacky angle. (You know the old expression, "Put your head down and run" —and it's right. You have to.) In the second case, you want to know where the fence is so you can judge how close you can get to it. If the ball is hit to the wall, you want to get that last inch of fielding room. You also want to be able to judge whether it will be wiser to play for the rebound.

But these are not exceptions to the rule because in any case you will always look back at the ball before it comes down. This is standard, down-the-middle operating procedure for outfielders because by the time the ball gets to the outfield and presents the problem of whether or not to look away, it'll be well hit...a ball that will stay up. Infielders have a different problem. You've seen a first baseman or catcher chase a foul ball to the dugout, looking away from the ball two or three or four times as he moves to gauge the remaining distance. And then you've seen that same first baseman or catcher tumble down the steps of the dugout chasing a foul because he never looked to see where the danger was. But, as I say, infielders have that special problem. In the first case, the ball was up long enough for the man to take his eye off it for a moment. In the second case, it didn't go that high in the air, and he had no choice but to play the ball 100 per cent.

You won't get that problem in the outfield. Some outfielders, even in the majors, still have trouble, though, relocating the ball once they take their eye off it. I've seen outfielders who purposely played deep so they wouldn't have to turn their back on the ball.

To lick this—and it's one of the most important things an outfielder can learn—I'd suggest that you start off all by yourself, just tossing a ball high into the air and catching it. Next, take your eye off the ball just as it starts coming down, for a split second. Then try looking away for a little longer period of time. And finally, start looking away *before* the ball gets to the top of its rise—that is, while it's still going up.

One more word of advice—start off with a tennis ball. You'd be surprised what can happen to your sense of timing the minute you look away. You'll look back expecting to see the ball still up there some fifteen feet and it'll be right in your lap. Or on your noggin.

The next thing to do—and here you *gotta* use a tennis ball—is get a buddy to throw some behind you. There's a basic rule to remember here. If you have to back up more than five steps to catch a fly ball, don't do it.

If you have to go farther back than that, or even if

97

you're in doubt, the thing to do is turn, run in a forward direction away from the ball, then turn again to face it. Watch your favorite shortstop as he goes into left field to catch a high pop-up. If he's got any kind of distance to travel, he won't back up.

There are numerous reasons for this. The first, and most simple, is the kind of arc a fly ball makes. The basic error that every kid outfielder makes twenty times or more is getting set for a fly ball and then at the last minute reaching over backwards because it's dropping behind him. And yet, you never see one dropping right at his feet. Why? Because if you mis-gauge a fly ball, you can almost always reach out in front of you at the last second to haul it in. If it's back of you, you're in all kinds of trouble.

You're in bad shape to make a throw, too, if you're backing up when you make the catch—especially since the ball is traveling in the same direction you are, and will add its momentum to yours.

But what it boils down to is simply this—man was invented to run forwards, not backwards. I dare you to go outside this very minute and run fifty yards backwards as fast as you can without losing your balance or falling over your feet or both.

All right. Now we've got this buddy of yours tossing fly balls behind you. In turning away from the ball in situations like this, you don't necessarily have to take your eye off the ball. We said, remember, that the only time you had to do that was when you needed that head-down posture for a long, hard run. Most of the balls hit behind you in the outfield will be not too far behind you and high enough to give you ample time to get there for the catch. So you can watch the ball as you drift over, never taking your eyes off it.

An incidental thing here is that a great many outfielders frequently time a catch so they don't get there before the ball does. They have the right idea. Even when a fly ball is hit so that I don't have to move to catch it, I try to stay in motion. I have sort of a tiny dance step I do with my feet, and I pound the pocket of my glove a couple of times or more. The reasoning behind this is that if you plant yourself to wait for a ball and something goes wrong—the wind takes it, or it falls faster and shorter than you'd expected—then it's somehow real tough to get untracked.

Also, if, as the majority do, you're catching the ball with your hands up in front of you, you're sometimes likely to put your hands up too soon and block your vision.

By this time, your buddy has probably tossed a couple of dozen up behind you. Now he's going to start throwing them farther back, so to get there in time you have to get your head down.

You should watch the ball just long enough to gauge its distance and direction. Direction is simple. If it's behind you to your left, turn left to go back. If to the right, turn right. Try to run "shoulder first"—that is, to go so that you will take the ball over one shoulder or the other. It's tougher to take a ball straight over your head because the human head doesn't turn on a universal joint. You can only look straight up so far back and then it doesn't go any farther.

If there is any margin of error in the course you take once your eye is off the ball, then it should be in the direction you turned to begin with. That is, if you turned to your left to start running away from the ball, the catch should be made out over your right shoulder. If you have to swerve or change direction, it should be to the right. You've seen an end in football muff a pass or miss it completely because he "turned the wrong way." Well, it works the same way in baseball. If you turn left to chase a fly and then have to turn left again to catch it, it means simply that you should have turned right to begin with. Making this play the wrong way frequently causes a player to trip or lose his balance. But at best it loses him a couple of steps.

Once you're grounded in the basics of this play, the only way to become good at it is to practice. Fungo hitting is a good way, with you camped in the outfield to make the catches. You'll find that gauging distance is something that only practice can teach you—but practice is a good teacher. It's not something you'll never be able to learn. With every ball you go after, you'll get better at it.

Line-drive hits are something else. They're not the toughest play an outfielder has to make, in my book— ground balls are. But many outfielders claim that making the play on the line hit is the toughest thing to do.

Two things make line drives hard. One of them is that all line drives—the kind that sail and the kind that sink— behave the same as they leave the bat. And if you wait to gauge them, frequently you're too late, because they don't stay in the air very long.

That in itself is sort of an advantage, though. As a basic rule, you can be pretty sure that a line drive isn't going to go over your head. Not the kind of liners we're talking about. Putting it another way, if it *is* going to be a long ball, you'll know it the minute you see it leave the bat. Some outfielders know it even before that—they can sense the long ball as the bat comes around. DiMaggio could. That was part of the "instinct" he was talking about. But notice, anyway, that I said you could tell when you *see* the ball leave the bat. That phrase "off at the crack of the bat" has no meaning for outfielders. Maybe some of you fans can tell whether a ball is a good shot or not just from the sound it makes as it leaves the bat, but any outfielder who waits for what the ball sounds like isn't long for his job. By the time the sound reaches him in the outfield, that ball has already traveled some fifteen feet. Add that distance to the distance the ball will travel in the time it takes the outfielder to react anyway to a line hit, and that man's in trouble.

Generally speaking, your troubles with line drives will be not so much the catching of them as the decision you have to make, in a split second, as to whether the ball can be caught at all. There's no golden formula here to solve this. Even Mickey Mantle frankly confesses he has all kinds of hardships with "those balls hit right at me."

You can take comfort, though, in a couple of things. One is that the play will be in front of you. Another is that if the ball is hit even slightly to the side, either way, of the line between you and the plate, it will be much easier to gauge.

One thing you will have to overcome, not only on line drives but on other outfield hits as well, is the tendency we all have to start forward, towards the infield, the instant

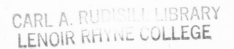

the ball is hit. Some young outfielders fight this to the ex-
tent that they go too far the other way and see the ball
drop ten or fifteen feet in front of them. But I'd suggest
your doing that too. A tendency to move back is easier to
correct than a tendency to move in.

Personally, I play a short center field. If you have got
speed, the ability to get a fast jump, and (by the way)
fast outfielders on either side of you, it is a good thing to
do, though there are and have been great outfielders who
didn't do it. Surprisingly, many people believe that I play
a shallow center field because my arm is strong enough to
make the deep throw when I have to go back. That makes
no sense at all, and of course doesn't enter into the situation. Your arm has nothing to do with where you play,
because it's not where you play but where the ball goes
that dictates how far you'll have to throw.

I think that playing in close is a percentage move. Generally speaking, an outfielder will have more balls to field
in front of him than behind him. Of course, the closer in
he plays, the less that is true. But on the other hand, by no
means all balls that are hit to the outfield are in the air—
even part of the way. You have to deal time and again with
ground balls through the infield. So by playing in close,
your percentage is good not only on the shallow flies that
so often fall for hits, but also on holding slow hits to a
single where a fast man might try for second.

This is to explain the center field I play, not to recommend it for everyone. And when I say I play a short center
field, I mean only a few yards difference between where
I play and standard depth.

And when Ted Kluszewski comes to bat, I'm as deep as anybody!

3. *Anticipate your play.* All this means is, decide *before* the ball is hit what you'll do if it comes your way. I not only do this—I sometimes overdo it.

In the last game of the 1954 world series, the Indians had men on first and second with two out in the last half of the seventh inning and the hitter singled to center. I'd already decided to throw home on such a play. I got the ball and heard Monte Irvin, in left field, holler, "Third base!" I hesitated, shifted my feet, and threw to third. I didn't get the man there, and of course the run scored.

I don't know for sure that I would have got the run at the plate; I'm not sure I would have got the man going to third; and, by the way, I'm not blaming Irvin. When you're ahead 7 to 3 with two out in the seventh, as we were, the relatively shorter throw to third, instead of the one to home, is probably the sounder play to make. Getting the man at third ends the inning, and the potential run at the plate is not a key run.

On the other hand, I think I would have had a good chance on that man going home, and that's what I'd decided in advance to do. I tell this story to illustrate the way I concentrate on making up my mind in advance. When I changed my mind in mid-play, I didn't get anybody.

Once again, let's face it—Willie Mays has still got some things to learn.

"Well," you say, "it's all very well to say make up your mind in advance, but how do you do it? How do you know what kind of ball he'll hit to you—fast or slow or in or out or to the side or whatever?"

The answer to that is, you don't know. So you do the logical thing. You set up the "crash" play in your mind. For example, let's take that play I outlined above in that world series game against Cleveland. Wertz was on second base and Jim Heagan was on first. Neither of them especially fast men. Two out. Last of the seventh. Giants ahead 7 to 3.

That's not all I thought of. Other things, such as who'd bat next in the order, the way they'd been hitting our pitcher, and so forth, also entered into it.

All right, I said to myself, *now if that man on second tries for home, then the man on first will try for third, so if I have a play at one base, I'll have a play at either base.*

There was something else to consider, too, and that was that the hitter, who was Rudy Regolado, might try for second base on a throw from me to third or the plate. In other words, conceivably a play might be made directly on him. I wasn't thinking of the infield cutting off a throw, because that would be up to the infield, not to me. But then I reasoned that with his club behind 7 to 3 in the seventh and two out, Regolado wouldn't be likely to take any chance on the bases.

Now all this reasoning was based just on one possibility —that Regolado would hit a single to me on which the man on second base, Wertz, would try to score. That's the "crash" play I was talking about. That was the only kind of hit that I had to think out in advance.

If he hit anything else to me, I had no worries in the

104

advance preparation department. A fly out would end the inning. A sharply hit single would hold Wertz to third and, of course, Hegan to second. A ball long enough to score Hegan from first would almost have to be a ball on which my throw went not to a base but to my relay infielder.

And any other hit—such as a slow grounder or a Texas Leaguer—would give me *time* to make a new decision to fit the way the play was unfolding.

So I didn't have to consider every kind of hit in the book to make up my mind beforehand. Assuming the ball was hit safely, and to my territory, I knew that the possibilities fell into four categories: (1) no play on a runner going for the extra base (because he didn't try for the extra base); (2) enough time to decide what to do; (3) a play that was up to the relay man to make, not me; and (4) the "crash" play. Number four was the one I doped out in advance.

Of course, you don't go through all that when you're actually in a game. What you do is simply size up the situation and then say to yourself, "If he hits it to me, I'll..." By that, you mean the "crash" play.

There are times when you have to consider a couple of different plays. With less than two out, for example, you have to reckon with a fly ball as well as a base hit. But it's something you do automatically. Always have your mind settled in advance. Get into the habit of saying to yourself, "If he hits it to me..."

Not only outfielders, but every player on defense should constantly be anticipating the play. That's why as soon as there's two out in an inning, you always see the catcher hold up two fingers so the whole defense can see. He's re-minding his teammates of that *next play*.

The alternative is the fielder who finds himself in the "crash" situation and has to think what to do. I don't blame people for thinking I had to stop and think when I fielded that ball in the Cleveland game. It certainly looked that way.

And it might as well have been that way, because I didn't get anybody.

4. *Know your hitter*. It used to be popular to say of the Philadelphia Athletics, after their pennant-winning teams, that all they had left was "nine minor-league players and one major-league score card." The score card belonged to Connie Mack, the manager. He'd sit there and wave it in one direction or another, and his outfielders would move accordingly.

Proper position play in the outfield is the one important defensive advantage that doesn't depend on talent. It will pay off time and time again, even against bad-ball hitters. (And any pitcher will tell you more base hits come on bad pitches than on good ones. Not that the bad pitches are any easier to hit—they're harder to hit. But you just can't set a defense in advance for what a hitter will do to a pitch that's not in, or very close to, the strike zone.) Wee Willie Keeler was a bad-ball hitter, and he said it all with his motto, "Hit 'em where they ain't." On our club Al Dark and Don Mueller are amazing the way they connect with bad pitches. I'll chase them, too.

As a general rule, though, your batter is going to hit most of the time to a certain area of the field. If he doesn't, it's usually because of the way he's being pitched.

A funny thing in the placing of the defense is that sometimes different clubs will set their men in noticeably different ways to defend against the same hitter. In this connection, you can bank on one thing. If different teams vary in the way they play a given hitter, he must be a pretty good hitter. The better he hits, the more different theories and experiments will be tried to defend against him. There's a man in our league—I won't use his name—who several seasons ago figured out the one pitch Stan Musial couldn't hit. It had to do with Musial's batting stance, the idea being that hitting as he does, with his right knee flexed, he would be off balance against one certain pitch.

It was only tried once. Musial hit it 450 feet for a home run.

The link between pitching and defense is far greater than most fans think. Again, the reason is that the defense sets against a hitter for *where he will hit where he is pitched*. This doesn't mean that you have to move fifty feet between every pitch. Except against a bad-ball hitter, your pitcher is not going to be moving the ball around willy-nilly. If you see a pitcher going from well inside to well outside against the typical hitter, you can assume that either his control is off or that one or two throws were waste balls. And the heavier the hitter, the more you can count on your pitcher throwing to certain spots rather than all over the map.

Confidence in the pitcher, such as the Giants have in Sal Maglie, is a great defensive boost. We *know* Sal's in there to make them hit it where we are. At the other extreme is the pitcher who decides to outguess the hitter on his own, without letting the rest of the team in on it. In that case, he's not only crossing up his catcher—he's working against his whole defense.

You've gathered by now that it's important for the outfielder to see the pitching signals. It is, although the more basic thing is knowing the pitching pattern. Remember, too, that a batter can get more "pull" on a curve ball than on a fast ball—and that hits that are "pulled" tend to hook, like a golf ball, in the direction of the "pull." Hits to the opposite field, on the other hand, tend to slice. In either case, you almost never see a long ball to right or left field that tends to curve in toward center. Many's the time you've heard of the likely home run that "just curved foul at the last moment." Outside of an occasional wind-blown fly, you never heard of one that "just curved fair."

Part of the science of knowing your hitter, by the way, is knowing the way he runs bases. You're always hearing about runners who will or won't run according to the way such-and-such an outfielder throws. But there's also the case—for example, a throw back to first base on a single—of an outfielder who will or won't throw according to the way such-and-such a runner runs.

Which brings us very logically to:

5. *Get rid of the ball!* If you don't do anything else, do this!

There is simply no play you can make by holding onto the ball. When we were kids back in Alabama, we played sandlot games and there was this one kid who played outfield and who'd field a ball and then run in towards the infield with it, holding it cocked as if he was going to

Left: Willie in the locker room after the game in which he took the lead in race for the 1954 batting title. *Right:* Willie at the age of 13, a picture taken in 1944. *International News Photos*

Willie's family at home in Alabama, including some of his stepbrothers and sisters. Standing, in the usual order, are Shirley, Uncle Ed Satterwhite, stepfather Frank McMorris, Anna Pearl. Seated are Nan, Charlie, Ernestine, William Edward, and Juanita. *International News Photos*

With his skipper, Leo Durocher. *International News Photos*

Scoring against the Yankees in the sixth game of the 1951 world series.
International News Photos

Willie on the base paths. In this crazy mixed-up play which happened in the seventh inning of a night game at the Polo Grounds, in April, 1954, Willie is being sat on by Dodger shortstop Reese. Dodger teammates Newcombe (facing camera), Campanella (39), Cox (3), and Hodges (14) were in on the play. During the rundown Lockman came around to third (top of the picture). *International News Photos*

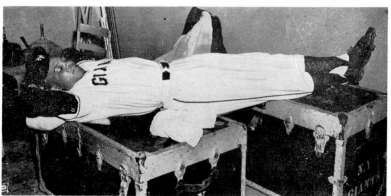

Relaxing in the clubhouse. *International News Photos*

Two ways to slide—head first and feet first. Safe both ways. *International News Photos*

The swing from start to finish. *International News Photos*

The basket catch in sequence. *International News Photos*

Manager Durocher's welcoming bear hug as Willie joins the Giants at Phoenix in the spring of 1954 after his discharge from the Army. Monte Irvin at right. *Wide World Photos*

A Mays special—catch of Duke Snider's long drive to deep center at Ebbets Field in August, 1954. Despite the catch and Willie's 37th homer, the Giants lost and their lead was cut to half a game. *Wide World Photos*

Private Willie Mays. *International News Photos*

Left: Willie as he appeared on a television show on the eve of the 1954 world series. He is shown at the window of his New York apartment at 80 St. Nicholas Place. *Right:* Crowning Dusty Rhodes after his three-run homer won the first game of the '54 series for the Giants. *International News Photos*

The Catch. In deep center, 450 feet from home plate, Willie hauls down Vic Wertz's drive in the eighth inning of the first game of the '54 series at the Polo Grounds. Cleveland manager Al Lopez said this catch, followed by a great throw, "broke our backs." *Wide World Photos*

Farewell till spring. With his bats and bag Willie takes a last look at the Polo Grounds until next year's opening day. *International News Photos*

throw. All that happened as a result of that was that the runners went right on running.

Practice getting the ball away in a hurry once you've caught it. (As I've said, that's one of the reasons for my "basket" catch.) I say once you've caught it and I mean once you've caught it. Throwing the ball before you have it is the surest way to make an error.

The bluff throw, which is standard procedure on certain infield plays (like a ground ball to short with a man on second, where the shortstop bluffs his man back toward second before throwing to first), doesn't belong in the outfield. The only exception here might be on a hard single on which the right or center fielder, seeing the hitter make a wide turn around first, bluffs a routine throw to second prior to a bullet pick-off throw back to first behind the runner, or actually bluffs the hard throw to first in an effort to make the runner dig for second. In the latter case, even if the bluff worked, it is likely that the runner could recover and get back to first when you threw to second base, so the only chance of getting him would be a rundown started by you as an outfielder. In either case, you would have to be quite close to the infield to give the bluff any authority. Nine times out of ten this kind of bluffing won't work. More often than not, it can cost you. The best advice here is what I said going in: Get rid of the ball!

If you are close enough in so that your throw can be made either on the fly or on one bounce, throw on the bounce. If there is no cut-off play in the works, it doesn't make much difference. I know a lot of baseball men feel that it is easier to handle a throw on one bounce than on the fly (for one thing, they say a bounce will come in lower, as a rule, against a sliding runner), but I think a good throw on the fly has no reason not to come in just as low, and you're protected against a bad bounce or skip. As a general rule, though, if a ball is deep enough for a runner to try for an extra base, you'll be throwing on the bounce just out of distance alone.

With the cut-off in operation, though, it's a different thing. You'll be throwing on the fly for the cut-off man, if you can reach him that way, and if he lets the ball ride through to third base or the plate, then it will get to the third baseman or catcher on the bounce. When the cut-off is a possibility, *never* throw for the distant base on the fly. It will make your throw too high for the cut-off man to handle if that's what he decides to do. Maybe he can get it by jumping for it, but if he has to go through contortions to bring the ball down he'll probably be too late to make the cut-off work. I stick to the advice I got early in my major league career—I aim on the cut-off man, knowing that he's right in a line between me and the far man.

The fielding of balls on the ground is most important. Balls that are hopping and skipping by the time they get to the outfielder are the hardest to get away fast. Fly balls or hits on the big bounce are, as a rule, easily handled. The ones that handcuff you are the grounders—not only because they're tough to play but because frequently you're not in position to throw.

The best position to be in for a throw is to be moving forward at the time you get the ball. You are not only in good position, but your body momentum adds zip to the throw (on flies and hits where you can get in front of the ball before it gets to you, you'll frequently see outfielders go a step or two farther back than necessary and then come forward to meet the ball, so they'll be throwing on their forward momentum). Personally, I don't often use the classic outfielding stance for fielding a ground ball, which is down on one knee. The theory behind this is sound. You are using your body to block the ball going through because there's nobody behind you to backstop. Maybe this became a popular thing with outfielders after the legendary experience of Smead Jolley, an outfielder with the old Red Sox, who had a hit go through his legs and rebound off the wall behind him. Jolley wheeled around to field the rebound and the ball went through his legs coming back, too.

In some situations, I will block a ball in the down-on-one-knee fashion even though I know there's no way I can get it away short of standing up again. Personally, I prefer whenever possible to play a ball infield-style. If I wasn't so hepped up on endless games of pepper and infield practice, I probably wouldn't feel as confident about it. I do make errors this way that I likely wouldn't make playing it safe. On the other hand, I think that over a season it works to the credit side in runners cut down and other runners who held up rather than take the chance. It possibly saved us a run in the first inning of the second game of the world series.

But I don't wish this on you as a standard piece of advice. It just happens to be the way I play it.

I'm unorthodox in another direction, too. All the experts say you should use two hands when you catch a ball. I think you should, too . . . but not for the reason they talk about. They say it's safer that way. I don't think safety is the key angle. The reason I like to use two hands most of the time is so my throwing hand will be where the ball is! I want to get rid of that ball like it's a hot coal.

There are other things about outfielding besides the ones I've mentioned, but I think those that I've talked about are the essential things. Some important things depend a lot on circumstances. The score can dictate what you do (like if you're tied and the other team has bases loaded and none out in the last of the ninth, you play in almost to second base). Playing caroms off the wall depends more on the wall than it does on you. And I suppose a whole book could be written on playing balls that more than one fielder can get to, but it wouldn't do any good. Any ball you can get to, you should try for. If it's clearly one man's ball, your teammates will yell it out even if you don't have the sense to pull up yourself. But there are any number of situations where two or three men have just about an equal shot at it. No matter how often you swear one of those situations won't happen again, the next time something's just a little different and you have a brand new set-up. Al Dark, Monte Irvin and I converged twice in one game—a big game, the one that clinched the pennant for us in 1954—on almost identical bloop hits back of short. Each time it started out looking, to the fans at least, like Dark's ball, but it carried out there, and one time I just missed a belly catch and the second time Irvin made a wild one-handed grab of it. Both times the three of us nearly killed each other.

The first rule I spoke of about outfielding was to be alert, and the more alert you are, the more times you and somebody else will be going for the same ball. Sometimes you wind up playing Alphonse and Gaston and nobody gets it. A couple of seasons ago, this happened to three New York Yankees. They grouped together in a tiny triangle and watched the ball drop among them.

The only thing you can say in a situation like that is that the man facing the ball should have preference because the play is easiest for him. But in practice that's not much comfort.

Once in a while your strength can be your weakness, there's no doubt about it. When I first came to the Giants, I had to concentrate on getting my throws down lower. I got them down so low and hard that they skip-bounced and were hard to handle. So I brought them up a bit again.

"And if it doesn't work this way," I told Dark, "get me a side order of spaghetti and I'll *eat* the ball."

Chapter 8

BABE RUTH, MOVE OVER

BEING a celebrity isn't quite the joyride it's cracked up to be.

It's tough to put it into words. I didn't really find out what it was like until halfway through the 1954 season.

And then, all of a sudden, I was expected to be something I'm not.

The biggest thing of all was, I was the new Babe Ruth. I was going to beat his record of sixty home runs in a season. I was 'way out in front of Ruth's sixty-homer pace in 1927. So that proved it.

I had an idea I *wasn't* going to beat Babe Ruth's record, but there wasn't any use telling anybody that. They'd say, "Oh, you're being modest," or they'd say, "Mays is playing it safe," or, "Mays is playing it cute."

"Look," I'd say, "I'm not out to break Babe Ruth's record."

"Maybe not," they'd say, like they didn't believe me, "but you're still running ahead of him, aren't you? What do you expect us to think?"

114

I don't know. Sometimes you got no answers at all.

Opening day of '54 I hit a home run against the Dodgers. I hit it off of Erskine, 440 feet into Section 35—one of my favorite places at the Polo Grounds. It's upstairs in deep left field. The homer came in the last of the sixth inning and broke a 3-to-3 tie, and we won the game 4 to 3.

I was pretty pleased. I don't remember what I thought exactly as I came around the bases. But I certainly wasn't saying to myself, "Okay, Willie, that's number one—fifty-nine more to tie the Babe."

It was a good start for the Giants, though. And the first time we played in Ebbets Field in '54, I homered again as Maglie beat the Brooklyns 6 to 3.

But if you think the Giants were off and flying, you've got another think coming. We lost a game to Pittsburgh by a 5-to-4 score when Whitey Lockman had a two-run homer taken away from him because time was out at the moment he hit it. Then Pittsburgh beat us again, 7 to 4, and you know where the Giants were?

Last place, that's where. The standings read one-two-three-four-five-six-seven-Giants.

We weren't going to stay there, though. There was one sure sign . . . we began to win the close ones.

We were tied with the Chicago Cubs in the fourteenth inning at Wrigley Field on April 30. It came my turn to bat against Warren Hacker. Leo Durocher said to me, "Watch for the high knuckler and tip into it."

Sure enough, there it came. I swung, and there it went for a homer.

On May 9, we saved a ball game from the Pirates when Al Dark turned a lousy throw of mine into a beautiful fielding relay that caught Preston Ward trying to score. On May 12, Bobby Hofman smacked a two-run pinch-hit homer in the ninth to win for us. In a game against Milwaukee, I had a double and a home run and batted in four runs.

On May 24, I got two home runs and drove in four as we beat the Phils 5 to 4. We went on to beat the Pirates 21 to 4 on twenty-two hits, then beat them 2 to 1. I homered again. We went in against the Dodgers and beat them 17 to 6. I homered, but so did five other Giants. Four of our home runs came in the eighth inning.

At St. Louis on June 3, we beat the Cards 13 to 8. I got two home runs and Henry Thompson got three. I batted in five runs and he batted in eight. We went on to sweep Milwaukee four straight. The fourth of those games was a wowser. In the seventh inning, I made a throw I'll remember for a long time, getting Henry Aaron at home after Bill Bruton had hit a long fly with bases loaded. The score was 0-0 at the time.

The game went to the tenth, and then Bill Taylor pinch-hit a home run for us. It was one of the longest clouts I ever saw. I think it must have traveled 500 feet.

By now we were neck and neck with the Dodgers for the league lead. I hit my seventeenth homer as Maglie and Hoyt Wilhelm combined to blank the Cubs, 5 to 0, and then we came back to the Polo Grounds. It was mid-June by now, and the Giant fans were in for a solid month of red-hot baseball play which to my mind exceeded even our sixteen-game winning streak in 1951. We didn't win any sixteen in a row this time, but we won most of our games—and you should have seen the way we won them.

Cincinnati was the first team in to face us on our home stand. They led us 3 to 2 with two out in the ninth. What happened? Henry Thompson hit a three-run homer to beat them 5 to 3.

The next day Jim Hearn pitched a four-hit shutout as we whitewashed the Reds 4 to o. Then we beat Cincinnati again, 2 to 1.

The Cards came in and Harvey Haddix shut us out 5 to o, but in the game after that Hoot Evers, an American League cast-off who'd been picked up by the Giants, got his only hit in a New York uniform. It was a pinch-hit homer with one out in the last of the ninth and the score tied 2 to 2. Evers didn't stay with us long after that, but after the world series the Giants remembered that one home run of his and voted him a $1,500 cash bonus from the world series cut.

On June 20, I was hitting .313. I was batting sixth in the order. Those two facts were to have considerable bearing on why, to the amazement of the fans, it seemed in the last half of the season that I'd just plain stopped hitting home runs.

Meanwhile, though, we were still winning them the hard way. In our third game against the Cards we trailed by 6 to 3, but in the sixth inning Hofman, Westrum, Dark, and Dusty Rhodes all hit home runs—Hofman and Westrum as pinch hitters!

I hit my nineteenth and twentieth home runs as we beat St. Louis 8 to 5 on June 21. Milwaukee was next in town, and we won another wild one. I homered in the first inning for one run, but we trailed 2 to 1 in the last of the ninth. I hit a double to score the tying run. And then, with bases loaded and two out, Monte Irvin came off the bench to pinch-hit. Monte had been hitless in his previous twenty-six times at bat. He promptly singled to center to win it.

We lost 5 to 2 to the Braves in our next game, but on June 24 I hit my twenty-third home run with one on in the second, and that was the ball game as Don Liddle beat Milwaukee 2 to 1. Now we led the league by one game.

It was a real hot night against the Cubs the next night. The first time I came to bat, I hit an inside-the-park home run to left-center.

And then something happened that hadn't happened to me since I was pitching in that sandlot game in Fairfield, Alabama. I got out to my position in center field for the next inning, and all of a sudden the Polo Grounds started to go around and around in circles. I had to call for time until the dizziness went away. Sure enough, the next hitter smacked a fly ball right at me. I made the catch, somehow. Then I went back to fighting off the heat sickness. We won the game, 6 to 2.

In this stretch, by the way, I'd hit six home runs in five games and five times in a row I'd homered my first time at bat. This wasn't going to keep up.

But the Giants were.

Wes Westrum slammed a base-loaded home run as we beat Chicago again, 6 to 4. In the next game against the Cubs, we were behind 2 to 0 with two out in the ninth. Then Whitey Lockman homered for two runs to tie it. And in the tenth, Bobby Hofman hit a pinch homer to win, 3 to 2!

That set up what may have been the most exciting

ball game of the season. The Dodgers were coming into the Polo Grounds for a three-game stand. We were leading them in the standings by one game.

Maglie was ahead in this one by a score of 2 to 1, with two out in the ninth and bases empty and a jampacked crowd rooting him on. Sal went ahead of Roy Campanella, no balls and two strikes. He wasted one inside. Then Campy caught the curve and rode it into the left field stands for the game-tying home run.

We went that way to the thirteenth inning. Then, in an identical situation—two out, none on, a 1-and-2 count—Don Hoak homered to put Brooklyn ahead 3 to 2.

By this time Wes Westrum had been replaced by Ray Katt as Giant catcher. But we got three walks to load the bases with two out in our half of the thirteenth, and manager Leo unhesitatingly called for Dusty Rhodes to hit for Katt.

And Dusty went to a 1-and-2 count, too. Then he slammed a base hit to center field.

Don Mueller was on third at the time. I was on second. Mueller would score the tying run, of course. If I didn't score the winning run behind him, we'd go into the fourteenth inning—without a catcher left!

Boy, you never saw anybody run so fast in your life as I did. I made it home, and we had the game 4 to 3.

I make a point out of this, because it illustrates Leo Durocher's thinking as a manager.

A reporter said to him in the clubhouse after the game, "That was some gamble you took, pinch-hitting for your last catcher. Suppose you hadn't won it and the game had gone into the fourteenth inning?"

"Who was thinking of the fourteenth?" Leo responded.

The next day, John Antonelli, with Hoyt Wilhelm in relief, beat the Dodgers 5 to 2. The day after that, the score was tied 2 to 2 in the last of the eighth when, to the consternation of apparently everybody, Leo sent Rhodes up to hit for—of all people—Monte Irvin.

Rhodes promptly whacked a two-run single, and we went on to sweep the series with a 5-to-2 win. The Dodgers were very vocal about that move Leo had made. "Any time they have to pinch-hit for Irvin, they must really be hurting," Roy Campanella said. I think they were a little sore because they just hadn't expected to see a left-handed hitter at that point, and as a result they had only right-handed pitchers in action—one on the mound and two in the bull pen. They were helpless to counteract Leo's sudden percentage move.

We ran our winning streak to eight in a row in our next game as we got five runs in the seventh to beat Pittsburgh 9 to 5. I had two doubles in that game. In the next game I hit my twenty-fifth home run, but the Pirates ended the streak with a 6-4 win.

Back to Ebbets Field now for three more with the Dodgers. I hit my twenty-seventh home run in the first game, my twenty-eighth in the second, my twenty-ninth and thirtieth in the third. We won them 5-2, 10-2, and 11-2. We led the league by 6½ games!

Against the Pirates on July 11, we again had a six home-run splurge. I got one to raise my total to 31. That was our last game before the All-Star Game break.

It was along about this time that a bunch of photographers got out a big piece of cardboard and pasted on it pictures of Babe Ruth (with the number 60 written in), Jimmy Foxx (58), Hank Greenberg (58), Hack Wilson (56), and Ralph Kiner (54). Those, of course, were the top single-season home-run hitters of all time. Then they had me sit there like that statue of "The Thinker," staring at those pictures and numbers.

It got so you couldn't take a shower without having a reporter or a photographer in there with you. The magazines started going to town on me. They even sent a team of photographers out to snap me in a stickball game with some kids on a street in Harlem.

My income was going up, of course. Television appearances and testimonials, all of them handled through the Art Flynn Agency, which takes care of such things for most of the Giants, were building up. You could tack those on to my base salary. There'd be a big world series check in, too, before the year was over.

They wrote some songs about me. My puss showed up on the cover of *Time* magazine.

One day, Frank Forbes said to me, "Well, boy, you finally made it."

"What do you mean?" I said.

"You're a real celebrity now," he said. "One of the gossip columnists says you're about to get married."

I achieved another kind of fame, too. One day I hit a home run at the Polo Grounds and they announced it over the loudspeaker at Ebbets Field. "Ladies and gentlemen," the announcer said, in a voice of doom, "just thought you'd like to know—Willie Mays just hit another one."

That didn't make much of a hit with either the Dodgers

or the Dodger fans. After all, they had a pretty good center fielder of their own, guy named Duke Snider, and according to the fans' own votes, he and not Willie Mays was the starting center fielder for the National League in the All-Star Game.

With all this going on, I think the Giants themselves did more to keep me on an even keel than anyone. On one of the home runs I hit, I got back to the bench and Leo suddenly turned his back on me and walked down to the water cooler at the other end of the dugout. I said to one of the other players, "What's the matter with him?"

"The bunt signal was on," the guy said. "Leo's mad as all get out."

Another time, I hit a homer and nobody on the whole bench would talk to me.

"It's all right," I said in a loud voice. "I know I hit one."

Then everybody busted out laughing.

Right after the All-Star Game, in which, by the way, I played part-way and didn't do much of anything, we shut out the Cards 4 to 0 back of Don Liddle while Brooklyn was losing a double header to the Milwaukee Braves. Our lead was up to seven and a half games.

In our next game against the Cards, I hit my thirty-second home run. But it was destined to be a bad road trip—for personal reasons, too. We lost that game 5 to 4. I left the line-up before the game was over. Word had come that my Aunt Sarah had passed away after a lingering illness.

Frank Forbes went back with me to Alabama for the funeral. I shut myself into a room at Aunt Sarah's house because there was a whole crowd of people there, and I think some of them were there just out of curiosity.

I rejoined the club in Milwaukee. Frank and I grabbed a cab at the airport in an effort to get to the ball park before the game there ended. It was at night, and either that cab driver was a Milwaukee fan or it's an awful long piece from the airport to County Stadium. Or maybe both. Anyway, I got there too late to do any playing. Just as I was getting dressed in the clubhouse, my old friend Bobby Thomson was hitting a pinch single to beat the Giants 3 to 2 in the ninth.

We lost three in a row to the Braves, then came back to New York and got beat 9 to 1 by the Dodgers. Our lead was down to three games.

On July 27, we lost to St. Louis 7 to 4. That game stands out in my memory because it was the occasion of what was probably the longest home run I ever hit. I hit it in the ninth inning. The ball landed in the stands upstairs beyond the bull pen in left field at the Polo Grounds, where the stands curve around to face home plate. I couldn't tell how far upstairs it landed, but at the base of the wall there it's about 440 feet.

And the thing about it was, Harvey Haddix threw me a change-up! It's tough enough to hit a fast ball a long distance. When you do it to a slower pitch, you've really done something. A baseball, remember, is essentially just a rubber ball. You take a rubber ball and bounce it hard off a wall. It bounces back a good ways. Throw it slow against the wall, and it just dribbles back at you. The same thing applies to fast and slow pitching. Lots of people don't realize this. They figure that the faster a pitch is

123

thrown, the more momentum the batter has to overcome before he can hit the ball back the other way. But think about that wall and that rubber ball again, for a minute. The wall had to overcome the ball's momentum too. And yet the harder you threw it, the farther the ball rebounded.

Maybe you wonder why pitchers throw fast balls at all. Well, think back on guys like Feller and Walter Johnson, and maybe you won't have to wonder.

That shot off of Haddix was my thirty-fifth home run. But now our lead over Brooklyn was down to two games.

The next day I hit my thirty-sixth homer as Antonelli beat the Cardinals. They say that right-handed hitters are less effective against right-handed pitching, but of those thirty-six homers, twenty-four came off right-handers. But that's not as strange as it sounds. The percentage of batters against pitchers is based on typical weakness against curve balls, and in that department I really had come along. I wasn't so hot on curves back in 1951. By now, though, I could hit them.

St. Louis beat us 8 to 0 the game after that, and a real storm let loose in the New York papers. Manager Durocher yanked Whitey Lockman out of the game and Whitey didn't like it and threw a couple of towels around. That's literally all there was to it. We'd been losing a little too much and nobody felt very happy about it, and it was one of those things that blow over almost before they even start.

But you should have seen the papers!

They said the Lockman episode was just one sign of the dissension that was running through the club. They hinted that Durocher wasn't even talking to two other players on the club. They said the Giants had fallen apart. At least one columnist came out and said flatly Brooklyn would win the pennant.

What happened next? We ripped off a six-game winning streak, including one against Cincinnati that Rhodes won for Johnny Antonelli with a pinch-hit home run.

At the start of that winning streak, Leo Durocher came to me and said, "Look, we've been losing and I'm putting you fourth in the batting order. You can get your average up if you'll start hitting to right field."

That was just about all there was to the conversation. But right there is the reason I hit thirty-six home runs up to then and only five more (and two of those were inside-the-park) the rest of the season.

Most people thought Durocher had told me just to "meet" the ball because by swinging hard I was striking out too much. He told me to "meet" it all right, but strike-outs had nothing to do with it. Being fourth in the batting order meant two things—first, I'd come to bat more often than I did when I was hitting sixth, and second, I'd have heavy hitters coming up behind me. The thing to do, very logically, in this new situation was to concentrate on getting on base. By swinging a lot for right field, I'd increase my chances because the defense would have more area to set against and worry about.

I believe that over a full season, the ability to hit to all fields can add a hundred points to your batting average. I really do.

Fans ought to pay attention to where a man hits in the batting order. It can mean all kinds of things. Some men are great in one spot and can't do a thing in another.

Some, of course, are especially qualified to bat in one particular spot, like, for example, a man who can get to first
base a lot and has speed—he's a natural to lead off.

The reason that the pitcher always bats ninth in the
order (or at least, in the majors he does) is not only that
most pitchers are weak hitters. That's true, of course, but
another thing enters into it very definitely. Of all positions
that change hands during a game, it happens most frequently to the pitcher. That's where you're most likely to
get a substitution. Thus the manager who has to change
pitchers for defensive reasons doesn't have to rip up the
strong part of his batting order to do it. Let's say you have
a good-hitting pitcher and you bat him fifth. The other
team knocks him out of the box, and your next pitcher
isn't a good hitter. He'll still bat fifth in your line-up.

Another thing to consider is that the farther down in
the batting order you are, the fewer times you'll get to
come to bat, over a season. Or even in a single game. The
two greatest out-and-out sluggers that baseball ever saw—
Babe Ruth and Ted Williams—batted neither fourth nor
fifth in their line-ups, though that's where you usually
find the heaviest hitters. They batted third. That way
they'd be sure to come to bat in the first inning, which in
turn meant they wouldn't have to lead off in the second.
And they increased their chances of coming to bat again
in the ninth (and that was something for pitchers to think
about before giving them an intentional walk). Next time
you're watching a close ball game, by the way, watch the
way a pitcher who's already got two out bears down to get
the man batting *ahead* of the heavy hitter. If he gets that
front man out, he not only gets out of the inning without

having to face the heavy man with men on base, but **he** gets another break too—the heavy man will have to come to bat next inning as the lead-off man, so there automatically won't be anybody on base for him to drive in.

Of course, in the case of Ruth and Williams, there were sluggers batting right behind them. Lou Gehrig and, for the most part with Williams, Buster Stephens. That was another good reason for pitchers not to give up intentional walks to Williams and Ruth.

A strong bench helps a batting order, too, much more so than many fans believe. The value of a good pinch hitter is not only that he's likely to get a base hit for you. The real value is that he can get it *when you need it*. So long as they're in the starting line-up, all the Ted Williamses in the world won't help you if you need a hit when it's not their turn to bat.

You can enjoy a game of baseball a lot more by watching the way a manager works in terms of his batting order —and the other team's, too. Sometimes a pitcher is on the rocks, and yet the manager lets him stay in to face one more hitter and then instantly brings in a relief man. That hitter may have been a left-handed batter, and maybe the next four men in the order were right-handers, so, playing the percentages, the manager wanted to wait out that one man before bringing in a right-handed reliefer. Or maybe he'll leave his pitcher in to stagger through the complete inning and then pinch-hit for him in the next half-inning. This frequently happens when the team is behind two runs or more. The reason is that the manager, looking ahead to his half of the inning, intends to pinch-hit for the pitcher anyway. If he relieves him the inning before, then he has to get another relief man ready to sub for the first relief pitcher whose place in the order was taken by the pinch hitter.

And if you don't think that pinch-hitting—and the manager's manipulations of his bench—have a lot to do with baseball, take a look at the Giants of 1954.

We won the pennant by five games.

Not counting other pinch hits, and there were many of them, pinch-hit home runs alone won the pennant for us.

We had ten of them.

Nine of them won ball games.

Chapter 9

BABE RUTH, MOVE BACK

MAJOR league pennant races can be wonderful things to sit back and watch. Sometimes they look like long drawn-out horse races. In 1950, for example, the front-runner (the Phillies) was obviously tiring and staggering at the finish, but just did hold on to win. In 1951, it was a hot horse (the Giants) coming from behind in the stretch to close with a dead heat.

And in 1954, all of a sudden, it was a three-horse race. The Milwaukee Braves, fifteen games out of it, suddenly couldn't lose for winning. We'd seen our lead trimmed to two games, you remember, only to step out again with a six-game winning streak. While we were winning, the Dodgers were dropping an entire series to the suddenly hot Braves. In one of those games, Joe Adcock of the Braves hit four home runs. He also got beaned by an inside pitch, and only his protective helmet saved him from what might have been a critical injury.

I feel the way most ballplayers feel about the inside pitch. I think there is a definite difference between the

129

pitch designed to keep the hitter from overcrowding the plate and the pitch designed to hit him, or even "low bridge" him. The difference lies completely, of course, in what the pitcher intends to do. Even the best pitchers can be off a little in their control. Even if you passed a rule that no pitch could be inside, lack of control would result in inside pitches. It's part of baseball. For a while, every time I came to bat I could count on the first or second pitch being so close I'd have to jump back. The pitcher hopes that once that's happened, the hitter won't stand quite so close to the plate, won't dig in quite so solidly, for the next pitch. The good hitter will go right back to his regular stance. Unless you're an out-and-out sucker for curve balls, any pitch that drives you back will be a ball, not a strike.

I do a great deal of first-ball hitting. Many players simply won't swing at the first pitch. Their reasoning is this: There are certain pitches, certain counts, on which the pitcher more or less has to get the ball over the plate— 2 balls and 0 strikes, 2 and 1, 3 and 1, and 3 and 0. Even on 1 and 0, the pitcher already is behind. On the 0-and-0 count, on the other hand, the pitcher certainly doesn't have to try for the heart of the plate. More likely he'll be trying for the corner, hoping the batter will either take the called strike or, in swinging, foul it off or get only a piece of it— at any rate, not a solid hit.

So the chances are rated as pretty good that in trying for that corner, the pitcher will miss, and the hitter, by laying off it, will be ahead on the count right away. At times, too, with men on base, a manager will have his hitter "take" the first pitch so he can watch the defensive pattern as the ball is thrown. Or if he senses a pitcher is getting wild, the manager will have his hitter lay off the first pitch—and, if the wildness continues, the pitches after that, too.

But of course it can work both ways. Some pitchers, gambling that the hitter won't swing at the first one, will fire it right in there and be ahead right away in the count. Next time you go to a game, watch for the pattern on the first pitch. Notice, too, that all of a sudden it'll seem like every man on the team is swinging for the first pitch. That can happen usually after the game is more than half over. By that time, the rival pitcher has decided his pitching strength. By that I mean that he has found what pitch is working best for him and by now, naturally, is relying mainly on that pitch. Most pitchers need at least two innings of actual work to find out about their best pitch that day. Very few can do it on warm-up alone. Some pitchers, like Maglie, still haven't even been able to discover an effective way to warm up. Sal has tried long warm-ups and short warm-ups, early warm-ups and late warm-ups, but he still usually needs that first inning or two of actual game conditions to reach his right pitching point. Game after game it's seemed like Sal had runners on every base against him the first inning, almost as bad the second, and then—boom! Nobody could even get to first base.

Anyway, you may find that your rival pitcher is getting ahead on the count all the time. He's getting that first strike over, so you're always hitting in a hole—o and 1, or o and 2, or 1 and 2. Watch for that pitcher who's getting ahead like that—and then watch how all of a sudden the other team starts first-ball hitting on him!

In my case, Leo rarely controls me at bat. I haven't become a good bunter, and in the past I have not often been under instructions to hit back of a runner. The result usually is that I can swing at what I want to swing at. If it's the first pitch, okay.

Babe Ruth could move back. His home-run record wasn't in any danger from me—not that it ever really was —as we stepped off our six straight as July ended and August began. I was swinging for right field now. Slowly but surely, my batting average was beginning to climb. And I was hitting more steadily than ever before. It was at this point that I started on a twenty-one-game hitting streak.

But all of a sudden a tempest hit the Polo Grounds. Milwaukee came in for a three-game series. And Milwaukee won all three games.

The Braves still were in third place, back of the Dodgers, and there's a very sound baseball theory that says it's better to be in second place ten games out than in third place five games out. When you're in second, you can concentrate on winning. For every game you win while the first-place team is losing, you've picked up a full game in the standings.

When you're in third place, though, two teams have got to lose every time you win for you to gain ground. By the time August comes around, you're really in trouble if you're third. For one thing, you've only got eight weeks of the season left to go, which isn't much time. For another, with the season two-thirds of the way through, two teams have been able to win more games than you have—which indicates that your competition is tough, and that even if one of those two should do a fold-up, it's extremely unlikely that both will fold.

But all of this was not much comfort to the Giants. We didn't care who was in third place or second place or forty-fifth place. We were going for that pennant, and here we were losing ball games.

I remember that particular part of the season for another reason. August 8 was Willie Mays Day at the Polo Grounds!

The fans really gave me a day. Among the gifts were: a deed for a suburban homesite, plus a covering check for $1,000; two sharp clothing outfits; an air-conditioning unit; three sets of luggage; a watch and other jewelry; a television set; the Ray Hickok athlete-of-the-month award; and a plaque from the *Amsterdam News*, which sponsored the event. The Polo Grounds ushers chipped in and presented me with a portable radio. And my team-mates gave me a record cutter. They knew my weakness for anything that had to do with a phonograph.

That didn't help our lead in the standings, though. Didn't hurt it either, of course, but the facts of life were these—on August 13 we led Brooklyn by only three and a half games. And Milwaukee was still closing in.

We went into Ebbets Field for a three-game series. In the first game, I singled for one run and scored another. But we lost the game 3 to 2.

We lost the next one 6 to 5, and the one after that 9 to 4. I wasted a ninth-inning homer in that last game.

We'd now lost four straight to Brooklyn—that 9-1 single

game after the All-Star Game (which was, by the way, the first time Maglie had ever been beaten at Ebbets Field), and now these three in a row.

And our league lead was down to half a game.

That night I had to go on television and do a happy dance while a bunch of guys sang one of the Willie Mays songs. I went through with it. I never was more miserable in my life.

What happened then? I got four hits as we beat the Phillies 8 to 3. We went on to sweep the Philadelphia series. I didn't get a single ball out of the infield in a long, tough double-header against the Pirates. But we won both games, 5 to 4 and 5 to 3—Bill Taylor pinch-hit the winning run across in the first game—and while that was happening, the Dodgers were losing two games to the Phillies! That marked the end of my twenty-one-game hitting streak, but I couldn't have been happier. I wasn't worried about a slump. We stared our final tour of the West, and in our first game, at Chicago, we beat the Cubs 5 to 1 for our seventh straight win. I got two triples and a double in that game.

We won more than we lost on the trip, and neither the Dodgers nor the Braves could hit a really hot streak. Coming back to the East, we had six games left with the Dodgers, three with the Braves. We were pretty happy about it. If we couldn't beat those two teams, we didn't deserve to win the pennant—and we figured we had the club that could win. Don Mueller and I both were beginning to move in on Duke Snider's league hitting lead. We had a strong bench. Our fielding was holding up. And as for our pitching—well, there were Maglie and Ruben

Gomez for right-handed starters. For left-handers there were Don Liddle and a fellow named Antonelli whose twentieth win of the year had been a four-hitter against the Cards at St. Louis on August 30. In the bull pen, we had the strongest relief staff in baseball, headed by Wilhelm, Grissom, and Windy McCall.

Our lead over Brooklyn was three games as we started our last series with them at the Polo Grounds. I've told about how Hoyt Wilhelm won his own game with a single in that one—a 7 to 4 victory for the Giants. That was the time where a sports writer asked me whether I'd win the batting title or the most valuable player award or both.

"Neither," I said. "I've never won anything like that in my life."

The game after that, we wrecked the Dodgers as Henry Thompson homered with bases loaded. They won the third game of the series, but now we led by four games with only three weeks to go.

In the two weeks that followed, the Dodgers were beaten four straight times by the Pittsburgh Pirates! The Pirates may have been dead last in the standings, but they never looked better than the way they handled the Brooklyns. And when the Braves, who'd actually been in second place for a day or so, came into the Polo Grounds for their final three games with us, we won all three.

We needed a victory over Brooklyn—just one—in the final series we played them at Ebbets Field, starting on the last Monday night of the season.

Sal Maglie pitched one of the great games of his career that night. He went all the way. Only a bloop hit by Gil Hodges that I just missed catching (and I should have had it—I started late on the wet grass and even then just missed holding onto it) kept Maglie from a shutout. We won the game 7 to 1. I got three hits.

We were a happy bunch in the clubhouse after the game. They made me drink champagne, of course, and I drank two glasses before the room started to go around.

By that stage of the season, of course, we all knew we were going to win the pennant. I sensed it the night Wilhelm won his own game with that single against the Dodgers—that was September 3.

But manager Durocher knew it well before that. He went on a television show and said, "We slipped back to a two-game lead at one point, and then we pulled in front again. Then we came back to half a game in front, and once again we pulled away. That was when I knew we had it. Any club that could do that had to be sound."

And, of course, neither Brooklyn nor the Braves could start a really long winning drive against us. The Braves had three different ten-game winning streaks during the season, but they weren't winning before or after those streaks. Contrast that with the way the Giants went in June and early July, where we'd win six in a row, lose one, win four more, lose one, win five more. Or, for example, the Giants of '51, who won sixteen in a row, also won thirty-nine out of forty-seven.

There was no loafing for me even after we'd won the pennant. Duke Snider and I were battling for the hitting title, and Brooklyn wasn't using Snider, a left-handed hitter, against left-handed pitching. But in the last few days Don Mueller caught fire for us and it was a three-way race.

"What a spot I'm in," Durocher told newsmen. "Several days ago I wouldn't have hesitated to pull Mays out of the line-up to help him clinch the batting title. The Dodgers were doing the same thing with Snider against left-handers. But with Mueller and Willie both in it, I can't play any favorites. They both have to go all the way and take their chances with Snider."

Going into the final Sunday of the season, the hitting picture looked like this:

	AB	H	B.A.
Mueller	613	210	.3426
Snider	581	199	.3425
Mays	561	192	.3422

I'd taken the batting lead the night we won the pennant from Brooklyn. Now, with one game to go, I was in third place—though not, of course, by very much.

Both Mueller and I were going against Roberts of Philadelphia. Snider would be hitting against a right-hander, Jake Thies of Pittsburgh.

In our final games, the Duke went hitless; Mueller got two hits in six trips; I got three in four—a single, double, and triple. Two of them, by the way, were hit to right-center field.

The final standing read:

	AB	H	B.A.
Mays	565	195	.345
Mueller	619	212	.342
Snider	584	199	.341

Notice that I got to bat nineteen times fewer than Snider and fifty-four times fewer than Mueller, even though we all played in just about the same number of innings over the season. There you can see the effect of my having batted sixth in the order over most of the early part of the year. I was actually tied for third in the league with Stan Musial for number of hits, and yet I won the batting title. Mueller's 212 hits were tops in either league, by the way.

My average had climbed twenty-five points since I started going for right field. I've said that hitting to all fields can put a hundred points on your average, and I really think it can, over a whole season. The later you really start to hit in a season, the tougher it is to boost your average. For instance, if you start off the season with one hit in two at-bats, your average will be .500. It's gone up 500 points, from zero. Two games later, if you've had two hits in eight trips up to that point and once again get one hit in two at-bats, *that* one-for-two will only bring your average up 50 points, from .250 to .300. So you can see how you can reach the point where you have to go crazy at the plate to actually make a real difference in your average—especially when you're at .335 or over, where one hit in three trips, which ought to satisfy anybody, not only can't help you—it actually *drops* your average slightly.

That's why that twenty-five point boost really meant a lot to me—and a lot in terms of what Leo Durocher told me when he advised me to start hitting to right.

Between that final game of the year and the start of the world series on the succeeding Wednesday, it seemed like we didn't have a minute to ourselves. All New York was

138

happy about the Giant victory. We had a ticker-tape parade up lower Broadway to City Hall. Manager Durocher refused to ride in the lead car of the parade, giving that honor instead to Al Dark and myself. "I never pitched a ball or hit one all season long," he told that huge crowd at City Hall. "All of these guys did it." He referred to me as "the greatest ballplayer I ever laid eyes on." I could have busted for being happy when he said that.

But there was not only the parade—there were a couple of clubhouse sessions on "booking" the Indian hitters and pitchers, and there was the taking of the team photograph, and there was the signing of endless baseballs as souvenirs, and there must have been five hundred television programs. Coming back from Philadelphia after the final game there, I went on the Ed Sullivan show, then raced in a cab over to the NBC studios to go on the Colgate program, which was the same hour as the Sullivan show. At 7:30 the next morning I was on the "Today" show and at 12:15 that night I was on the "Tonight" show.

There was one advantage to those television appearances. I didn't have to worry about what to wear. I like colorful clothes, but with a conservative cut—not "zooty"—and I like to wear button-down shirts without a tie. I really dislike wearing ties. There was always a problem whether I ought to wear one on TV, but it almost always was solved, because the television people almost always requested me to show up wearing my Giants' uniform. So it was a double pleasure. I not only like to wear the uniform, but I didn't have to worry about a tie.

The funny thing about those shows was, though, that

almost everywhere I went I got the feeling that people were feeling a little sorry for us.

After all, we Giants were the poor lambs being led to the slaughter. We had to play those terrible, horrible, man-eating Cleveland Indians in the world series.

They were supposed to have better pitching and better hitting, and they were especially favored because it would be a short series.

Yes, sir, the New York ball club was just like a chicken that was about to have its neck wrung off.

Like that man Winston Churchill said one time, Some chicken . . .

. . . Some neck!

Chapter 10

LO, THE POOR INDIAN!

I'LL stake you right now the 1954 world series is going to be remembered for a long, long time.

Remembered by me, anyway . . . and not particularly for what I did in it.

I'm not unhappy about the way I went in the series against the Indians. I only picked up four hits, but three of them drove in runs; and some whiz on statistics told me afterwards that I figured in more scoring innings than any player on either side. If you figure it on a basis of doing one or more of these three things—scoring a run, advancing a runner so that he could score as things progressed, or batting in a run—then, the statistician said, of the eleven innings in which the Giants scored during the series, I figured in eight. Henry Thompson figured in seven. Henry had one world series for himself, let me tell you. Maybe that's what statistics are worth.

But I remember Leo Durocher coming up to me before the series began. He said, "Willie, I want to tell you one thing. They're going to be laying for you."

"I know it," I said.

"Play your game," he said, "and don't worry about anything."

"I got enough to worry about to start worrying about worrying," I said.

"Okay," he said. The truth of it is, I just wasn't worried about the series. If I had to tell you a hunch, without any way of proving it, I'd have to say I don't think the Skip was worried either.

Oh, we were 8-to-5 underdogs, all right. Among friends, it was 2 to 1.

But don't forget, we knew those Indians. The Giants and Cleveland have been kissin' kin in the springtime ever since the year one. Every spring they come north together from training quarters, playing exhibition games all the way up.

So we'd seen those Indians. Matter of fact, we'd beat 'em pretty good on the spring.

As players on a big league ball club, we didn't sit down in a big circle and dope the Indians, like the papers might have you believe we did. We knew we could match them —probably figure to do better than them—in fielding and running bases. As for hitting and pitching, we were just as glad to take our chances. For one thing, in a short series like the world series always is, with nobody else left to play once it's over, you can throw season's averages out the window. For another thing, we had each other scouted like nobody since Davy Crockett and the Indians—the real Indians—were swapping notes.

That's what Leo meant when he said to me, "They're going to be laying for you." I had the hitting title in the

142

National League, and I represented power from the right-hand side of the plate, and those Cleveland right-handers knew everything they could know about me. Besides, I had every right to expect that they'd be bearing down on me.

For that reason it happens so many times in the world series, a guy like Ted Williams won't hit, but somebody you're not thinking of will hit like wild roosters. Your pitcher in the series, with all the chips on the table, is going to come "up" for the big hitter.

And so it was in the '54 series. The hitting heroes were one guy on each side—Dusty Rhodes for the Giants, where everybody was laying for Mays, Mueller, and Dark—and Vic Wertz for Cleveland, where everybody was watching Doby, Rosen, and Avila.

That doesn't necessarily mean that the big guys can't produce a thing. The Indians sure were watching out for Don Mueller, and he still picked up seven hits. Al Dark picked up seven on his own, too.

But that big long ball came off of two bats—Dusty's and Wertz's.

We knew one thing, going into that '54 series—the Indians weren't going to beat us in the newspapers. Better than two-thirds of all the sports writers picked Cleveland. They said the Indians had won a record 111 games in their own league, and they said the Indians had the pitching, and they said pitching is what wins the world series.

Well, they were sure right about Cleveland winning those 111 games, because Cleveland did. And generally speaking, they were right in saying that pitching wins the world series.

143

But that left a good bit to be wrong about.

The Indians, in their league, had beat the socks off of five teams and just broke even against the other two—who were the White Sox and the Yankees. Since the league finished one-two-three Cleveland-New York-Chicago, with nobody else over .500, it'd be no more than fair to say the Indians did better against bad clubs than good ones.

Not so the Giants, though. You know something? We had six good clubs in our league (St. Louis, in sixth place in the National, won more games than Boston, in fourth place in the American). Six good clubs, and the other two could beat you. Last-place Pittsburgh only won 53 games on the year, losing 101, but they beat the Dodgers four times straight in the big end of the pennant race.

There wasn't a team in the league the Giants didn't beat on the season. Fourth-place Philadelphia was our best cousin—we beat the Phils 16 out of 22. We took 15 each from the Cubs and Reds, 14 from the Pirates, 13 from the Dodgers, 12 each from the Braves and Cards. That meant Milwaukee and St. Louis were the only two teams in the National League who beat us as many as 10 times on the year.

And don't let anybody tell you we didn't see good pitching in the National League. We saw Roberts and Simmons, Erskine and Podres, Nuxhall and Haddix and Rush and Spahn and Conley. And sometimes we'd face tough pitching five and six games in a row, where we'd move from St. Louis to Milwaukee and on to Cincinnati, say. In the other league, the two teams Cleveland had a tough time with—the Yankees and the White Sox—were in different divisions, eastern and western. That meant the Indians weren't liable to have to face those two teams hand-running; and *that* meant that generally Cleveland could count on having its big pitchers ready for any given series.

The Giants weren't so lucky, but how anybody could run down our pitching, I just don't know. Our pitchers had to go against hitters like Musial and Repulski and Moon and Mathews and Adcock and Crandall and Pafko and Sauer and Kiner and Ennis and Hodges and Snider and Kluszewski and Bell and Thomas and Furillo.

But the Giant pitchers, as a staff, turned in 64 games in which the other club was held to two runs or under! Sixty of those games, we won! And since we won 97 games all told, you can figure that pitching certainly took 2 out of every 3.

The Giant pitchers tossed 19 shutouts on the season. And 22 one-run games.

So how anybody was going to stand up and knock the Giant pitching, I'll never know.

I don't even want to know.

I know Leo sent Maglie in the first game of the series at the Polo Grounds September 29. There was a big house there—a record for a world series in the Giant park—52,751, it came to.

There was all the color and the music and the flags and the excitement. I got posed sixty-seven times with Bob Avila of the Indians before the first game. Avila had won the hitting title in the other league, and I was told this was only the third time in all the history of the world series that the two league batting champions had met head-on in the series. Cobb and Wagner faced off in 1909 and Chick Hafey and Al Simmons in '31.

The way Avila went his first time at bat, I had no reason to doubt he'd won his title. For Maglie, that first inning was a Maglie first inning. At that, despite having runners on, he almost beat it without getting scored on.

He went 3-and-o on Al Smith, Cleveland's lead-off man, and then hit him with ball four. Avila got a single to right, and when the ball bobbed away from Don Mueller, Avila went to second and Smith to third.

The fellows who'd made the odds favoring the Indians in the series never looked more right—before or after.

Sal got Cleveland's big men, Doby and Rosen, to pop up to the infield, but then Wertz drilled a long ball to right-center just when it looked like Maglie was out of the inning. The hit went for three bases and Cleveland had a 2 to o lead.

I had a good chance to get a hit in the first inning. I mean, it would have been a good spot for one because with one out, Dark had walked for us and Mueller singled him to third. But the best I could do was sky to George Strickland, the Cleveland shortstop, on the outfield grass.

We didn't score till the third. Then Whitey Lockman opened with a single and went to third when Dark singled through the middle. Whitey scored while Mueller was hitting into a force play, and after I'd walked on four straight pitches, Henry Thompson rammed the score-tying single to right.

And that was it—a 2 to 2 ball game, inning after inning. They were hitting Maglie, but they weren't scoring off of him. They had a man on second with one out in the fourth—men on first and third with two out in the fifth—a man on third with one out in the sixth.

Then, in the top of the eighth, Doby walked to lead it off for Cleveland and Rosen beat out an infield hit.

Up stepped Mr. Wertz, who'd tripled in the first, singled in the fourth, singled again in the sixth.

Leo relieved Maglie with Don Liddle, and the minute I saw Wertz's bat come around on Liddle's pitch, I was running. It was a whale of a ball. I had my back to the plate, running for the bleachers in dead center. The arc of the ball brought it down about ten feet or less short of the bleacher wall—probably less if it'd been allowed to fall to the ground. My glove was up and I had it, on the dead run, 460 feet from home plate. Red Smith wrote the next day that I'd been running for five minutes—it sure seemed that way.

The big thing here was to turn and get the ball away. Luckily, I was able to do that before I went sprawling. Davey Williams took my throw back of second and held Doby to a one-base advance.

Now the managers of the two teams started throwing the book at each other. Al Lopez of the Indians announced Hank Majeski to hit for Dave Philley, so Leo countered with bringing in Marv Grissom to pitch for us. At which point, Lopez turned around and had Dale Mitchell go up to hit for Majeski. And Mitchell worked Grissom for a walk to load the bases—with only one out.

You never saw anybody pitch like Grissom then. He got a called third strike on pinch hitter Dave Pope, and then Monte Irvin went to the wall in left to wait for Jim Hegan's long, high try—and that got us out of the inning.

147

We'd been doing practically nothing with Bob Lemon of the Indians all this time, and the trouble was all one-sided. Came the top of the ninth and the Indians had two men on again. Again, Irvin caught the inning-ending fly ball.

It was in our half of the ninth that Durocher made a move characteristic of Leo as a manager. The pitcher—by this time, Grissom—was supposed to be first at bat. Any other home-team manager might well have gone for the pinch hitter—especially if, like Durocher, he had the pick of the bench, with no one having been sent up to hit for anyone else so far in the game.

But Leo whacked Grissom on the seat of his pants and sent him out there to hit for himself.

We didn't score that inning, but, maybe strange to tell, we had something of a vision on our club along about then. We had a feeling it was going to go our way.

If it hadn't, it would have been strictly my fault. That same Vic Wertz was leading off for the Indians in the top of the tenth, and, watching from center field, I could see Grissom pitching him carefully, all the time on the outside. Wertz got one real mean foul to the wrong field, out to left.

I should have known to move over from right-center, but I didn't, and Wertz then slammed one up the left-center alley.

It was the toughest chance I had all world series long. That ball was mean as it hopped on the ground, and I had to play it at an angle. I speared it one-handed and held Wertz to a double with my throw.

The sacrifice moved him to third, and now Grissom

walked Pope to put on the force and get at the right-handed Hegan. Lopez sent up Glynn to hit instead, and Grissom struck him out swinging.

Again, Durocher made a move. Lockman, at first, was holding Pope close. Leo came to the steps of the dugout and waved Whitey a few steps off the bag—and Lemon lined the ball right smack into Lockman's hands for the third out.

There was one out in the bottom of the tenth when I came up. I'd noted that Mickey Grasso, who went in to catch for Cleveland in place of Hegan, had taken only one warm-up throw to second base. (Later, the papers quoted me as saying Grasso hadn't thrown to second at all, which is incorrect.) Anyway, that one throw he took was on the bounce. So I asked Leo if it would be all right to try to steal if I got on. He said sure.

I did get on. I got a walk off of Lemon. Sure enough, I went down on the steal, and sure enough, Grasso's throw bounced in and I had it beat.

Now Lopez decided to put the force on by handing an intentional walk to Thompson. That gave us men on first and second with one out and Monte Irvin due up.

Leo didn't hesitate an instant. Here came Dusty Rhodes. Here came Lemon's pitch. There went the ball—a pull fly ball that just did land in the near right field lower deck.

Tagging up on second, I saw Larry Napp, the umpire, signal the homer, and I guess I must have looked a little silly coming around the bases. First, I jumped up and down, clapping my hands, and then, thinking that maybe Thompson hadn't seen Napp's sign—the ball had bounced off a fan's chest and back onto the playing field—I started signaling to Henry like a traffic cop as me and him and Dusty came around the bases.

We had the opener, 5 to 2. Funny, though, it didn't convince anybody of anything. The Giants still were no better than even money for the series, and everybody was talking about Rhodes's "Chinese" homer—a kind of talk that might have been okay if it wasn't for the fact that we hadn't needed a home run at all. A single would have won it for us just as well.

In the Cleveland dressing room, Al Lopez said the catch I'd made off Wertz in the eighth was "the greatest catch I ever saw," but he was just using the old sheep dip, maybe like by way of saying that it took the greatest catch he ever saw to beat his team. Next day he was saying maybe it wasn't the greatest catch he ever saw.

Nobody said anything, though, about the way I played Wertz's double in the tenth—nobody except Maglie, who came over in the clubhouse after the game and said, laughing-like, "How come you didn't catch that one too?"

I said, "I'm sorry, Sal," and I meant it. I should have had it.

The Indians had left thirteen men stranded in that first game. Confident of our chances though I was, if anybody had come to me and said the Indians were going to leave thirteen more the next day, I would have told them they were whacky.

Johnny Antonelli went for us, Early Wynn for them in the second game, a misty, overcast set-up that held the crowd "down" to 49,099.

Right away we're back in trouble. Al Smith hit Johnny's first pitch for a home run.

LO, THE POOR INDIAN!

Everybody reached for the record book. It was only the third time in series history that a lead-off man had homered—and the first time anybody could remember that it happened on the first pitch.

In a way, it was good for us that it happened that way —simply because it happened so fast. It had sort of an unreal quality to it, like it hadn't really taken place. Antonelli took care of the next two hitters in fine style.

He was pitching carefully, though, and he lost the next two hitters—Rosen and Wertz—on bases on balls. Up stepped Wally Westlake, and rammed a hard single to center. I charged it, took it gloved-handed, and threw head-high to Westrum at the plate. The crowd went "Ooooh!" and after the game was over, Lopez again paid me a tribute. He said my play on Westlake's hit, which caused third base coach Tony Cuccinello to have Rosen stop at third base, was the "key play." I don't know. For one thing, Antonelli pitched out of the inning by getting Strickland, the next man, to pop to Lockman. For another, Rosen was hobbled by a bad hip and just couldn't run. There's no second-guessing whether or not my throw would have had a fast man, though Lopez swore no one could have beat it.

We got out of that inning, like I say, as though there hadn't been a run scored. But Cleveland had that big "1" on the scoreboard to remind us of what Smith had done to Johnny's first pitch, and as the innings went by, that "1" got bigger and bigger.

We didn't get a runner to first base off of Wynn for the first four innings. Over the same period of time, Antonelli had given up two more hits and two walks, and was helped by two great plays behind him—one by Al Dark on Rosen in the third and another by Thompson at third in the fourth. Henry literally threw himself to his left to nab Avila's hot shot, came to his feet, and got the ball in time to first base!

This is not to say, though, that Antonelli was playing it lucky. The box score would show that he struck out nine men during the course of the game, and he was showing Cleveland a kind of pitching they didn't see in their league too often.

I heard that Joe DiMaggio was sitting with a friend back of home plate, and that when Antonelli struck out Westlake to end the Cleveland fifth inning, DiMag—quiet, dignified, unexcitable—turned to the friend and said, "*Mama mia!*"

I remember that fifth inning for another reason. We'd been twelve up and twelve down against Wynn up till then, and I was leading off—and I got a walk.

Talk about cashing your opportunities—Henry Thompson instantly smashed out our first hit, a rifle single to right, that sent me to third.

And, batting for Monte Irvin, here came Dusty Rhodes!

He blooped the ball back of second. Watching it, watching Larry Doby as he came in, I knew it was going to fall in, and I took off, scoring the tying run without a play. There was a play on Thompson legging it to third, but he beat the throw. Rosen immediately whipped the ball back to second, but Rhodes, running all the way, beat *that* throw.

It was a real picture-book play for Giant fans.

Wynn bore down to get the next man, and then the

LO, THE POOR INDIAN!

Indians played it by the book, walking Westrum to load the bases and get at Antonelli. It almost worked, for Johnny hit a double-play grounder at Avila. But he was a step ahead of the relay throw at first base, and Thompson scored that run that put us ahead 2 to 1.

We were feeling pretty good on our bench along about that time. Leo, who'd been pacing up and down like a caged lion, stopping at the water cooler every four minutes for a drink, allowed himself to grin all around like a happy cat or something.

But if somebody had come down the dugout steps at that moment to tell us that the Giants would never be behind again in the whole world series, I swear Leo would have killed him.

We had this ball game, though. Antonelli started going to his fast ball more and more. In the eighth inning he struck out Philley and Hegan, and in the ninth he fanned Doby swinging for the third time after the Indians had put the first two runners on.

Nobody ever pitched more carefully than Antonelli did to Wertz, last man up for Cleveland in the ninth and already possessor of a single and two walks in that second game. At long last, Johnny got Wertz to hit high to left field. Rhodes, with lots of room, camped under the ball for the final out—which was really appropriate. Dusty hadn't only singled in the tying run as a pinch hitter in the fifth—left in the game, he homered next time up, leading off our seventh, to give us our eventual margin of victory —3 to 1 was the score. In fact, Dusty got two of the four hits we got off of Wynn. Cleveland got eight off of Antonelli, and six walks, but left another thirteen. Johnny wouldn't give them that big hit when they had to have it.

Incidentally, there were two things to take note of about Dusty's homer. First off, it certainly wiped out any "Chinese" labels he may have won from the first game, because this one smacked over the right field roof—a real belt of a hit.

The other thing is this: When the Indians finally did get Rhodes out, late in the third game of the world series (though not until he'd broken it open for us with another pinch hit), they did it by striking him out twice with bases empty. So after the game somebody said to Dusty, "How come you can't hit when there's nobody on?"

"I don't know," Dusty said, "I guess it must be that I just feel so lonely."

Then somebody else said, "You didn't look very lonely when you hit that home run with nobody on in the second game."

"Well," Dusty said, "maybe that was a mistake!"

But that gets me ahead of the story.

We got to Cleveland for the third game, and the shoe was supposed to be on the other foot. We were playing in the Indians's ball park, and it was their crowd yelling at us, and things were going to be different.

By golly, things were different—about as different as they could be.

We'd won those first two games hard in New York. In Cleveland, we won the last two easy.

The Indians had scored in the first inning of the first game and again in the first inning of the second. So maybe it was a jinx that we scored our first time at bat in the third game at Municipal Stadium. But that big crowd

—it was 71,555—didn't seem to think so. And let me tell you a secret. Neither did we.

Least of all me, because I finally got me a hit. Lockman singled off of Mike Garcia's opening pitch. Al Dark went down swinging, but Strickland, playing short for the Indians, hurried a double-play throw to first on Don Mueller's ground ball to Avila. The ball went by Wertz, and Don was on second with two out.

I got a late-swing single to right for my first series hit, and Don rode around to score.

So we were ahead 1 to 0. Came the top of the third, and Dark led off for us. Mike Garcia wasn't going to strike him out two times hand-running. Alvin singled to left center.

Then came a play that was as beautiful to watch as any in the entire series. Cleveland could remember how, in the first inning of the first game at the Polo Grounds, Alvin and Don Mueller had pulled the hit-and-run, with Mueller hitting the ball back of Dark and into right field.

The Indians weren't having any of that this time. Dark lit out for second on Garcia's pitch, and this time second baseman Avila stayed right where he was, letting Strickland go over from short to take the catcher's throw. In addition, Garcia had the pitch outside, so Mueller couldn't pull it to right.

Mueller didn't. He slapped it to left, right through the hole vacated by Strickland.

It was the hit-and-run with the ball going *ahead* of the runner! And the Indians were so flabbergasted they didn't even have a play on Dark steaming into third base.

As base runners go, they don't make them any better than Al Dark. He proved this on the very next pitch—

Garcia's first pitch to me, which I hit hard, but on the bounce square into the hands of Al Rosen at third.

Dark was caught off third base, an easy rundown victim. But Al didn't run. He made them come to him. He danced between fielders along that third base line long enough for Mueller to make it to third and me to second—both of us standing up without a play.

Men on second and third, one out—that called for the automatic walk to Thompson to load the bases. And, just like it was an act, that's what the Indians did and bang!— here came Dusty Rhodes out of the dugout to hit for Irvin.

All Dusty did was to slam Garcia's first pitch to right field for a two-run single! That sent Thompson to third, and Davey Williams brought in Henry with a wonderful squeeze bunt. Garcia finally threw to first, but threw it high, and they didn't even get the hitter on the play.

You got the idea that the Cleveland fans were getting a little unhappy along about now. Garcia finally got Westrum and Ruben Gomez to end the inning, and he got a real Bronx cheer from the stands. No, let me change that. I think the fans were landing on the team as a whole, not on any one man.

Outside of walks to Smith and Philley, Gomez didn't give Cleveland a hit until Doby singled in the home fourth. But a Dark-Williams-Lockman d.p. took that runner off the bases. In the fifth, Philley got a lead-off single and stayed there as the next three men went down. Cleveland was behind by 5 to 0 by now, because in the top of the fifth, we'd scored another run.

With one out, Henry Thompson got a hit to center

156

field. It was a routine base hit, and the fielding was routine —neither especially bad, nor especially good. All the Indians knew was that by the time the ball was at second base, Thompson was at second base too. It was a double. He'd hit a single and just kept running.

And that kind of base-running meant a run, because Henry raced home from second on Westrum's two-out single to left and that was that.

And we made it 6-0 in the sixth. Lockman walked, Dark bunted him ahead, and with two out I lodged another base hit to right to bring Whitey around.

Up to the last of the seventh, Gomez had a two-hit shutout going. Then Wertz teed off and whaled the ball to right-center. I had a bead on it, but I never got there. That small fence that surrounds the outfield at Municipal Stadium in Cleveland got to me first.

I was so mad—mainly at seeing Ruben's shutout taken away from him where there would have been outfield room, and plenty of it, left in the Polo Grounds—that I shook the fence with my bare hand.

They picked up another run in the eighth—again, one they probably shouldn't have had. Glynn pinch-hit a double that Mueller got to but couldn't hold, and then we let them have the run. No reason not to. We were ahead 6-1. Dale Mitchell grounded out to Lockman, with Glynn going to third, and Dark threw to first on Smith's grounder, letting Glynn proceed homeward.

But Al's throw was off, and Smith made second on the error. Gomez then walked Avila, and Leo came out to the mound.

It was a hot, terribly muggy day in Cleveland, and

Ruben's sinuses were acting up. He was actually having difficulty breathing. So Leo made a claw with his hand, like Captain Hook, and that was the signal for the knuckle-ball man, Hoyt Wilhelm, to come in from the bull pen.

Here's what Hoyt did on the last five Cleveland hitters of the game, the first two of them coming up with two on in the eighth:

Ground ball, strike out, strike out, ground ball, ground ball.

It was as easy as that.

Oh, I got my third hit of the game in the top of the ninth—a single to center that moved Mueller, who'd singled leading off, to third. But nothing came of it. Thompson lined viciously to Strickland, and I was doubled 'way off first. There was an example, by the way, of how the situation and the score can dictate what you do. If we hadn't been ahead 6 to 2 in the ninth, I would have been a lot more cautious on taking off on a hit. The way things stood in this game, though, it was worth the chance.

The Giants had taken three in a row from the vaunted Indians now—each game easier than the last—and the base-ball world was stunned. We'd outfielded them and out-run them on the bases, but aside from that, we'd outhit them only by three hits—23 to 20 at this point. And they'd had 37 base-runners to our 28.

Let me suggest here, just a mild little suggestion, that maybe pitching had something to do with the way we were going! The pitching we had in that world series was something out of this world—all the way through.

LO, THE POOR INDIAN!

In the clubhouse, manager Durocher didn't have much to say after that third game. To one newspaperman who was congratulating him loudly, the Skip said, "How many games to win the world series?"

"Four," the guy said.

"We've won three," Leo said.

And he was right, of course. No matter how jubilant we felt like acting, we still had another ball game to win. It would take four losses in a row for us to drop the series —but we'd lost four in a row during the season. We knew it could be done.

The best way to keep it from happening now was to win the fourth game of the series. There was a 78,102 crowd at Municipal Stadium—it was a Saturday—and Don Liddle was going for us against Bob Lemon, coming back for Lopez after his grueling ten innings in the Wednesday opener.

The crowd was pulling for a miracle now—a miracle for the Indians, just as three short days before Giant fans were pulling for a miracle for us.

And the crowd wasn't left in doubt very long.

Henry Thompson walked to lead off the second inning for us. The Cleveland crowd—whose biggest yell of joy (or of anything, for that matter) had come the previous day when Dusty Rhodes, who'd stayed in the game after his pinch single, finally struck out—was expecting to see Dusty now.

But they saw Monte Irvin, batting for himself, instead. And Monte rammed a double to left-center.

With men on second and third, Davey Williams lined out to Wertz. Wertz had a potential double play on Irvin scrambling back to second, but his throw was wide. Thompson scored and Irvin went to third.

Then Westrum hit a medium-depth fly ball to right field. Irvin was poised to break for the plate on the catch. Westlake was in such a hurry to get his throw home that he threw the ball before he had it—almost literally, that's what he did. The ball bounced out of his glove for an error, and Monte romped in.

Williams made a great fielding play on Rosen's ground ball to start the second inning for the Indians. Then Wertz doubled, but that was all for them. As a matter of fact, they didn't have another hit till the fifth.

Meanwhile, the Giants were busy. Third inning, one out: Dark singles; Mueller singles him to third (right field this time!); I chop a double to left and we're ahead 3-0.

Then the top of the fifth, and here we go again. Dark and Mueller single back-to-back and I walk. That's all for Lemon. Hal Newhouser comes in, walks Thompson to force over a run. Again, the fans look for Rhodes, but again it's Irvin (Monte was looking for Rhodes, too!— looking back over his shoulder at the dugout as he came up to hit). And Monte singles for two more runs. Two sacrifices, and a fourth run is across, off of Ray Narleski, the third Cleveland pitcher of the inning.

The Giants were ahead 7 to 0.

We got a little careless in the Indians' fifth. With two out, there were two errors, setting the stage for a pinch homer by Majeski that gave them three runs. And they got another in the seventh on three singles.

After the third single, Leo relieved Liddle with Wilhelm, who got Dave Pope to end the inning with a ground ball back to the mound.

And then there happened one of the strangest sights in a world series game or any other game of baseball...

A pitcher actually was taken out of the game because he was too good!!

It happened in the Cleveland half of the eighth inning. Wilhelm started off by striking out Avila. At the point where Avila swung and missed at the third strike, the ball was in the strike zone. At the point three feet farther where West Westrum was waiting for it, it was so high over Westrum's head that Avila not only made it easily to first base—but the official scorer had to give the error not to the catcher but to Wilhelm, the pitcher!

Doby then flied out to me in center, and here Rosen got a looping single to left.

There was nothing wrong with Wilhelm's stuff—except that now there were two runners on, and a passed ball could mean real trouble. And as great a fielding catcher as Wes Westrum had to confess he was having trouble holding that knuckler.

Durocher had Antonelli and Grissom both ready in the bull pen. The Skip and Al Dark talked it over, along with Westrum and Wilhelm, and the call went out to the left-hander, Antonelli, to face Vic Wertz.

Face him? Antonelli struck him out swinging.

Westlake up now. Two out.

Called strike three.

Westlake knew it, too. Never said a word.

Just for good measure, with one out in the ninth, Johnny struck out pinch hitter Dave Philley, too.

Dale Mitchell, a real favorite with the Cleveland fans, batted for Pope with two out in the Cleveland ninth.

And he popped a little foul up the third-base line.

Henry Thompson came tearing for it so fast he lost his cap—something I do all the time, but he does rarely. Out in center field, I was saying to myself they couldn't have hit it to a righter man to end the world series with. Henry had scored six times in the series, more than any other man. He'd fielded like a madman—including one sensational start of a round-the-horn double play in this final game, back in the third inning.

Henry didn't catch that final ball. He squoze it. He hung onto it, not wanting to open his glove and look to see if it was really there.

Which of course it was.

The newspapermen were disappointed in us. They said we should have whooped it up more in the clubhouse after the game.

I don't know. Maybe we should have. Best thing I remember after that last game was on the plane coming back to New York (where there were 2,500 fans waiting at LaGuardia to greet us). Somebody came down the aisle of the plane with a bottle and some glasses, and he leaned in on me and said, "Say when, Willie."

"What is it?" I said.

"Champagne," he said.

"When," I said.

Chapter 11

GAME TIME TOMORROW

Everybody's always after me to list my "greatest" this and my "greatest" that, even when I tell them it's not my business to set up like a judge in a courtroom.

If I had to pick out one hit that gave me my biggest kick —I mean a hit *I* made, not counting the Thomson homer in '51—I'd have to vote, I guess, for the first major-league hit I got—that home run off of Warren Spahn.

My best play in the field? I don't know. I made a play in Pittsburgh that was along the same lines and just as much of a long run as the catch I made off of Wertz in the world series. The throw on Cox in '51 was a big one. I remember, too, a ball Solly Hemus of the Cardinals hit in St. Louis late in 1954. We were tied in the last of the ninth, and the Cards had Joe Cunningham, a pretty fast man, on first base with two out; and Hemus hit one off the wall in right over Don Mueller's head. I came over and got the ball off the wall and got the long throw to the plate on one bounce in time to get Cunningham. That was a real game-saver except for one little thing . . . we went on to lose the game.

That's baseball, of course. It all goes into making it the great game it is. I said back at the start that I liked baseball because it was the only sport besides tennis that doesn't have a clock or some other kind of measurement on it, so that whether you win or not is left up to you. That doesn't mean I'm falling-down nuts over tennis. Tennis, like so many other sports, has boundary lines. Football, for instance—maybe a guy will make a terrific catch in football and he'll be ruled out of bounds. In baseball, there are foul lines, of course, but that doesn't keep the play confined inside the lines. The only thing that can stop you when you chase a ball is that grandstand. In baseball, too, you don't have the penalties like you have in other sports. With rare exception, the only penalty you run into is getting thrown out of a game by an umpire—which hasn't happened to me yet—and that doesn't change what happened on the field or on the scoreboard. And finally, in baseball the scoring is simple and fair. Ain't no winning by a missed extra point or anything like that. No ties, either. If nobody's won it, you just go right on playing. And for every man that crosses that home plate, you get a "1" on the scoreboard.

You tell me a sport that can match it.

I've been asked time over time, too, to pick an "all-star team" or something like that from the guys in our league. That's ridiculous. I haven't got the experience, for one thing. For another, you ought to remember that there are no bums in the major league. They're all good. Or they wouldn't be there.

It's been good to me, baseball. When you counted up salary and world series money and testimonials and appearances and royalties, this young fellow from Fairfield, Alabama, did nicely in 1954. Everyone, from President Horace Stoneham of the Giants on down, treated me fine. Once the series was over, we Giants split up a record melon in which the full individual shares came to $11,147.90 apiece. For four games of baseball.

Boy, it was some autumn. Tallulah Bankhead wrote a magazine piece about me and Bill Corum wrote that I was the greatest natural ballplayer he ever saw, all in the same week.

And as time wore on there were the awards as Most Valuable Player in the National League, Major League Player of the Year in the *Sporting News* (the weekly baseball newspaper), Male Athlete of the Year in the Associated Press poll, and the Hickok Belt.

Wow!

I'd agreed to play for a team our coach, Herman Franks, had organized in Santurce, Puerto Rico, once the season was over. First, though, I took time off to go home for a few days and see the family.

Since the death of my mother, my half sister Anna Pearl has become "the mother." All told I have eight half sisters —Anna Pearl, Shirley Ann, Rose Marie, Jeese Rue, Juanita, Nan, Ernestine, and Diana; and two half brothers, Charles Frank and William Edward. Helping them out, seeing that they get the schooling they want, is part of my job.

Of course, we didn't talk about that much. Mostly, the kids wanted to know what about breaking Babe Ruth's home-run record.

I think Babe Ruth's home-run record will be broken, the same way they broke the four-minute mile in track.

I don't understand baseball men who say it's impossible for someone to hit 60 home runs—or 61—in a season. It can't be impossible—otherwise how would you explain the fact that so many have come so close? Foxx and Greenberg had 58 each, Wilson had 56, Kiner, 54.

As to whether I'll break Babe Ruth's record, well, it would come as a terrific surprise to me if I did. The 1954 season illustrates that I was more effective swinging for all fields instead of pulling for the fence. It's true that as a right-handed hitter, many people think of me as being at a disadvantage. My 41 homers in '54 set a new Giant record for the number of home runs by a right-handed swinger. The old record was 35, set by Walker Cooper. But the reason a right-handed hitter is supposed to be at a disadvantage is mainly that he faces mostly right-handed pitching. In my case, though, the great majority of my home runs in 1954 came off of right-handed pitching. They say, too, that left-handed hitters have an advantage in the home-run distances in most ball parks. Ruth was a left-handed hitter.

Well, Foxx and Greenberg were both right-handed hitters. Prove something.

I think the one thing that will make Babe Ruth's record stand up the longest is the pressure it puts on the man who's trying to break it. Most of Ruth's homers came late in the season—his biggest single month in his record year of 1927 was September. And at the time, he didn't have the pressure on him of having a record like that to shoot for.

But the pressure today is tremendous. Not only on the field, but in the stands and in the newspapers. One New

York paper was running a box score on me vs. Babe Ruth in 1954 before the season was even half over. And I don't care how relaxed you are. You're bound to feel something like that.

I go for the way Leo Durocher puts it: "Swing for the base hits. The home runs will come."

Relaxation is, I think, the one key to going good in baseball—in most other things too. It will help you most when you find you're not hitting as much as you should ... it'll be a big thing, in other words, in bringing you out of a slump.

It may sound corny, but I'd have to say, too, that living right is a very important thing. I don't like to drink or smoke. I do like to sleep. I don't have to watch my diet—I gained only five pounds all the time I was in the Army. *Feeling* good is important.

And you have to *want* to play baseball. That's why it was such a lot of fun for me to take off after the world series and go down to Puerto Rico to play ball in the winter sun.

Some magazine did a little story on what it was like for me playing down there, and they told about the fans in Puerto Rico, who really get excited about their baseball.

"Not long ago," the story said, "a cop caught a razor-blade salesman handing out free samples in the San Juan stands." And, the story added, "Puerto Rican fans have never been known to shave between innings."

Just before I left for Puerto Rico, one of my buddies said to me, "Well, you can take it easy down there. Play a couple of innings each game and then rest."

I said, "Are you kidding? Boy, they really come after you down there."

He laughed at that. "Well," he said, "looks like you got to go nine no matter where you are."

I don't mind it at all.

Sports Shelf Biographies
You Will Enjoy

Sandy Koufax: Strikeout King
by Arnold Hano

Willie Mays: Coast to Coast Giant
by Charles Einstein

Mickey Mantle: Mister Yankee
by Al Silverman

Ken Boyer
by David Lipman

Ted Williams
by Ray Robinson

Stan Musial: Baseball's Durable "Man"
by Ray Robinson

My Ups and Downs in Baseball
by Orlando Cepeda with Charles Einstein

Roberto Clemente: Batting King
by Arnold Hano

Willie Mays was aided in his writing chores by his friend Charles Einstein, a baseball writer and long-time Giant rooter. Mr. Einstein has been a sports writer for International News Service and is the author of countless short stories and articles.